She Can STEM

She
Can
STEM

50 Trailblazing Women in Science
from Ancient History to Today

LIZ LEE HEINECKE

QUARRY

Quarto.com

© 2024 Quarto Publishing Group USA Inc.
Text © 2024 Liz Lee Heinecke
Illustrations © 2020–2023 Kelly Anne Dalton

First Published in 2024 by Quarry Books,
an imprint of The Quarto Group,
100 Cummings Center, Suite 265-D,
Beverly, MA 01915, USA.
T (978) 282-9590 F (978) 283-2742

Quarry Books titles are also available at discount for retail, wholesale, promotional, and bulk purchase. For details, contact the Special Sales Manager by email at specialsales@quarto.com or by mail at The Quarto Group, Attn: Special Sales Manager, 100 Cummings Center, Suite 265-D, Beverly, MA 01915, USA.

10 9 8 7 6 5 4 3 2 1

ISBN: 978-0-7603-8606-4

Digital edition published in 2024
eISBN: 978-0-7603-8607-1

The content in this book was previously published in *The Kitchen Pantry Scientist Biology for Kids* (Quarry Books 2021) by Liz Lee Heinecke; *The Kitchen Pantry Scientist Chemistry for Kids* (Quarry Books 2022) by Liz Lee Heinecke; *The Kitchen Pantry Scientist Ecology for Kids* (Quarry Books 2023) by Liz Lee Heinecke; and *The Kitchen Pantry Scientist Physics for Kids* (Quarry Books 2022) by Liz Lee Heinecke.

Library of Congress Cataloging-in-Publication Data is available.

Design and Page Layout: Megan Jones Design

Printed in China

To each woman, famous or unseen,
who paved the way for women in science.

And to those treading the road today
to make a better future for all of us.

CONTENTS

INTRODUCTION 9

11 TAPPUTI-BELATIKALLIM
Fragrance
Distillation

12 MARIA SIBYLLA MERIAN
Biological Illustration/
Metamorphosis

15 LAURA BASSI
Air/
Electricity

16 EUNICE NEWTON FOOTE
Greenhouse
Gases

19 FANNY HESSE
Agar Growth
Median

20 AGNES POCKELS
Surface
Tension

23 MARIE CURIE
Elemental
Extraction

24 SUSAN LA FLESCHE
PICOTTE
Public Health/
Houseflies

27 MARY AGNES CHASE
Agrostology/
Grasses

28 YNÉS MEXÍA
Plant Collection/
Identification

31 LISE MEITNER
Nuclear
Fission

32 ALICE BALL
Organic
Separation

35 GERTY CORI
The Cori
Cycle

36 KATHARINE BURR
BLODGETT
Thin Films

39 CECILIA
PAYNE-GAPOSCHKIN
Star Material

40 DORA PRIAULX
HENRY
Barnacles

43 MARIA
GOEPPERT-MAYER
Nuclear Shell Model

44 MARY GOLDA ROSS
Aerospace
Engineering

47 RACHEL CARSON
Environmental
Contaminants

48 CHIEN-SHIUNG
WU
Symmetry

51 ANNA JANE HARRISON
Organic Compounds/
Ultraviolet Light

52 RUBY
PAYNE-SCOTT
Sunspots

55 ROSALIND FRANKLIN
DNA
Structure

56 MARGARET S. COLLINS
Zoology/
Termites

59 ESTHER LEDERBERG
Lambda Phage/
Replica Plating

60
EDITH FLANIGEN
Molecular
Sieves

63
TU YOUYOU
Medicinal Plant
Compounds

64
JUNE ALMEIDA
Coronaviruses/
Agglutination

67
SYLVIA EARLE
Ocean
Research

68
ADA YONATH
Ribosome
Structure

71
WANGARI MAATHAI
Green Belt
Movement

72
PATRICIA BATH
Medical Devices/
Cataract Surgery

75
CHRISTINE DARDEN
Aircraft Wing
Design

76
MARGARET
CAIRNS ETTER
Crystallography

79
VALERIE L. THOMAS
Illusion
Transmitter

80
JOCELYN BELL
BURNELL
Pulsars

83
LINDA BUCK
Olfactory
Chemistry

84
ROBIN WALL KIMMERER
Plant Ecology/
Traditional Knowledge

87
DANA BERGSTROM
Antarctic
Research

88
APARAJITA DATTA
Seed
Dispersal

91
LISA SCHULTE MOORE
Prairie
Strips

92
NADYA MASON
Conductivity/
Carbon

95
DANIELLE LEE
Pattern Recognition/
Science Communication

96
RAYCHELLE BURKS
Colorimetric
Sensors

99
LESLEY DE SOUZA
Conservation
Biology

100
AYANA ELIZABETH
JOHNSON
Marine Conservation/
Public Policy

103
JODIE DARQUEA
ARTEAGA
Bycatch Reduction

104
CHANDA
PRESCOD-WEINSTEIN
Cosmology

107
RAE WYNN-GRANT
Carnivore Ecology/
Animal Behavior

108
BURÇIN
MUTLU-PAKDIL
Galaxies

ACKNOWLEDGMENTS 110
ABOUT THE AUTHOR 111
ABOUT THE ILLUSTRATOR 111
INDEX 112

 Biology   Chemistry   Ecology   Physics

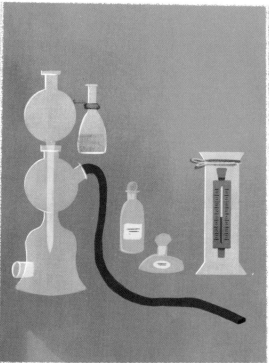

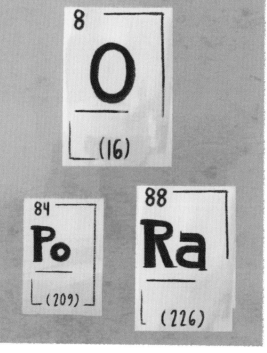

INTRODUCTION

When you think of a scientist, what image pops up in your mind? Do you picture an old man with crazy hair? That's how the world has been portraying scientists for a long time. Luckily, the face of science has changed dramatically and is continuing to evolve. Today, everyone should be able to see themselves as a scientist.

Women have been involved in STEM (Science, Technology, Engineering, and Math) for thousands of years and today, there are more women than ever working in these disciplines. This book lays out the biographies of 50 amazing women who are part of the scientific landscape, from historical scientists to modern ones. Many are role models who have inspired other girls and women to chase scientific dreams.

For example, in 1898, a physicist named Marie Curie became interested in invisible energy given off by some rocks. She figured out how to measure the energy and named it "radioactivity." Soon, she and her husband Pierre discovered two new radioactive elements and named them radium (Ra) and polonium (Po). Marie then invented a method to purify radium and won two Nobel prizes for her work, one in physics and one in chemistry. Few females did science at that time, but when girls and young women read about Marie's work, they realized that they could be scientists too.

Another scientist featured in this book helps us imagine how it might have felt to be the only woman in a large physics class in the 1960s. Day after day, Jocelyn Bell Burnell was harassed by fellow university students who stomped their feet, whistled, and banged on their desks as she walked through the lecture hall. In 1974, Jocelyn was the first person to discover spinning dead stars called radio pulsars, but she was left out when two men she worked with won a Nobel Prize for her discovery.

For centuries, women in STEM struggled to gain recognition for their work. In the 1700s, Laura Bassi (p. 14) was not allowed to lecture in public without the permission of men. In 1925, Cecilia Payne-Gaposchkin (p. 38) wrote a paper based on her research showing that the sun is made of hydrogen and helium. Two male astronomy professors told her she was wrong and then took credit for the discovery when they realized she was correct. In 1957, the physicist Chien-Shiung Wu (p. 48) was ignored when a Nobel prize was awarded to two men whose theory she had confirmed by designing and performing a complicated physics experiment.

Despite the obstacles, women like these overcame significant hardships to make groundbreaking contributions to STEM fields. Their curiosity, passion, and perseverance made a difference. By reading about the modern scientists in this book, you'll see that, although things still aren't perfect, people who love science are no longer limited by their gender. Each biography also includes an activity, if you'd like to get a better feel for the science behind the stories.

Next time you picture a scientist, I hope you'll think of Raychelle Burks, Danielle Lee, Robin Wall Kimmerer, Lesley de Souza, Chanda Prescod-Weinstein, or one of the other brilliant scientists whose stories appear in these pages. Because once we move past the image of an old man with crazy hair, the sky is the limit.

Tapputi-Belatikallim

FRAGRANCE DISTILLATION

ROYAL PERFUMER

Over 3,200 years ago in ancient Mesopotamia, a pen made from a reed inscribed the name Tapputi-Belatikallim in a soft clay tablet. Today the cuneiform notches and figures remain, and scholars who can read the ancient script tell us that she held an important post as the manager of the royal household. Thanks to the scratches in baked clay, which held its form as the centuries rolled by, we understand that Tapputi, whose second name means "overseer," prepared fragrances for the king and his family. The royals used some of the scents she prepared as perfume and saved others to offer to the gods during religious rituals.

MESOPOTAMIA

Ancient Mesopotamia lay between two rivers, the Tigris and the Euphrates, in a land known as the Fertile Crescent where Iraq and parts of Iran, Syria, and Turkey are found today. The fertile land gave birth to the first known cities: agriculture arose on the land, people began to domesticate animals, and written language developed. Mesopotamia was a center for culture and language and gave rise to the wheel, the chariot, and the writings of a high priestess named Enheduanna, the world's first author known by name.

TRANSCENDENT SCENTS

When Tapputi made her mark as the world's first recorded chemist around 1200 BCE, tendrils of fragrance were intertwined in social order, religion, and medicine. Tapputi and her contemporaries believed that the invisible, beautiful scents they offered could transcend the physical world to reach their gods, who would be pleased by their sacrifice. Kings were self-proclaimed conduits to the gods, anointed with the most valuable perfumes, while fragrant ointments and salves were used by healers as well.

ROYAL RECIPE

Tapputi's recipe for a perfume included preparing a mixture of oil, flowers, and a lemon-grass-type herb called calamus and then steeping the mixture with other fragrant substances before filtering and distilling it again and again. The distillates and oils she created served as salves and perfumes for the king. Her complicated, multi-step extraction method was recorded around 1200 BCE. An ancient copy of her recipe includes the first description of a distillation apparatus ever recorded and a number of her methods are still used today in modern perfume production.

IN TODAY'S WORLD

Chemical engineers use several of the same techniques that Tapputi used, but on a much larger scale, to create today's fragrances.

TRY THIS AT HOME!

Crush a fragrant flower. Breaking the plant cells open releases scent-laden molecules called essential oils. These oils are volatile, which means they quickly evaporate into the air.

Maria Sibylla Merian

BIOLOGICAL ILLUSTRATION/METAMORPHOSIS

AN ARTIST

Maria Sibylla Merian was born in Germany in 1647. She was encouraged to paint and draw by her step-father, an artist, who specialized in painting flowers. At that time, women didn't pursue the study of nature, but painting, drawing, and embroidery were considered acceptable hobbies for girls. Maria proved exceptionally talented at drawing the plants and insects she collected.

A NATURALIST

A curious child, Maria started investigating insects when she was young. Her life took a new turn when, at thirteen years old, she learned to raise silkworms. As she observed their metamorphosis from caterpillar to moth, she wrote, "I realized that other caterpillars produced beautiful butterflies or moths, and that silkworms did the same. This led me to collect all the caterpillars I could find in order to see how they changed."

METAMORPHOSIS

Maria married and had children, but she continued to paint. Besides teaching other young women to draw, she learned to make copperplate engravings of her illustrations so that they could be printed on paper. It was important to Maria that she accurately represent the color of the plants, insects, and spiders in her work, so she hand-colored many of the prints she made herself.

CATERPILLARS

After years of work, Maria published two volumes of stunning illustrations of the life cycles of the caterpillars she'd studied. Other artists had drawn butterflies before, but she was the first to accurately depict their entire life cycles, including where butterflies and moths laid their eggs, which plants certain caterpillars ate, where they could be found, and every step of their development, including molting. Her drawings highlighted the differences between males and females of different species as well, depicting butterflies from different angles to aid in identification. The book was popular with the public but ignored by other naturalists, because she had used common names rather than Latin descriptions.

SURINAME

When she was fifty-two, Maria became the first European woman to travel independently to South America to study insects. In the country of Suriname, she observed and drew insects, reptiles, amphibians, and plants. When she returned home after three years, she published a book of illustrations based on her observations there. Many illustrators and naturalists were hugely influenced by her work and Carl Linnaeus used her drawings to identify more than a hundred new species, including a bird-eating spider, which was later named *Avicularia merianae* in her honor. Maria has several butterfly species named after her as well.

IN TODAY'S WORLD

Entomology is the modern name for the study of insects and how they relate to the environment and other living things. Insects can be both helpful and harmful. Understanding the life cycles of insects is essential to modern scientists studying everything from agriculture and medicine to solving crimes.

TRY THIS AT HOME!

Search for caterpillar eggs, caterpillars, and chrysalises. Photograph them on their host plants and draw or paint them.

Laura Bassi

AIR/ELECTRICITY

A DEBATE

Europe's first female university professor, Laura Bassi, was born to a middle-class family in Bologna, Italy, in 1711. She was the only surviving child in her family, and although she never attended school, she was tutored in math, languages, literature, and natural philosophy from the time she was five years old. Although girls were not treated equally at that time, people recognized that she had an extraordinary mind and Laura was invited to publicly debate four professors from the University of Bologna when she was only nineteen years old.

MINERVA

At twenty, Laura became the first woman to receive a doctoral degree in science from the University of Bologna, and was made a professor at the same time. She was a celebrity. Several paintings commemorated the occasion, along with a bronze medal featuring Laura's face. People called her Minerva of Bologna, after the Roman goddess of wisdom and learning, and scholars and other travelers came from far and wide to meet her.

A LABORATORY

Although she was a professor and a member of the Italian Institute of Science, Laura was not allowed to lecture in public without the permission of men at the university. Because society would allow her more freedom to converse with other scholars as a married woman, she agreed to marry the physician Giuseppe Veratti. He had promised via letter that he would not "hinder her in her studies." She set up a laboratory in their house, where she taught and did experiments. Laura Bassi had eight children, but there were no vaccines against childhood diseases and three of them died very young.

AIR AND ELECTRICITY

As an experimental physicist, Laura Bassi was fascinated by the discoveries of Sir Isaac Newton. She was especially intrigued by his work with light and sometimes did public demonstrations of his experiments. Because she was interested in the relationship between light, air, and electricity, some of her own experiments involved studying bubbles that formed in liquids, and whether they were attracted to the walls of containers due to electrical forces.

A FORCE

Laura and Giuseppe had an "electrical machine" in their laboratory that made it possible for them to do groundbreaking research at home. They conducted dangerous experiments on atmospheric electricity at their country house, after experiments with lightning were banned in the city of Bologna. Laura authored at least twenty-eight papers in her career. Most involved Newtonian mechanics, but seven of her papers were focused on electricity. She exchanged letters with Alessandro Volta, who created the first battery. Volta was a great admirer of her work.

A CHAIR

When Laura Bassi was sixty-five, she was finally named the chair of physics at the University of Bologna. She died two years later at the age of sixty-seven.

IN TODAY'S WORLD

Static electricity is used in some factories to remove pollutants from smokestacks and pipes. Tiny particles can be charged and then exposed to a metal collection plate containing the opposite charge, which pulls them out of the air before it enters the atmosphere.

* PHYSICS *

TRY THIS AT HOME!

Pour carbonated liquids, such as soda, into clear containers with different shapes. Observe how bubbles form on tiny scratches in the glass and plastic.

Eunice Newton Foote

GREENHOUSE GASES

A FAMOUS RELATIVE

Eunice Newton was born in 1819 in Goshen, Connecticut. She had six sisters and five brothers, and her father was a distant relative of the famous scientist Sir Isaac Newton. Eunice grew up in Bloomfield, New York, and attended Troy Female Seminary, which is now called the Willard School. She took chemistry and biology classes at a nearby science college, where she learned about physics and chemistry.

SUFFRAGETTE

Newton married Elisha Foote, who was an inventor, mathematician, and judge, and they had a daughter who would grow up to be an artist, writer, and social activist. In 1848, Eunice attended the first women's rights conference in America and signed a document called the "Declaration of Sentiments." Written by Eunice's friend Elizabeth Cady Stanton, the declaration called for equality with men and the right for women to vote.

AT-HOME SCIENTIST

During the nineteenth century, only sixteen physics papers were published by American women and two of those papers were written by Eunice Newton Foote. Although she didn't have a lab, Eunice did science at home. She was interested in many things, including how sunlight interacted with different gases. Using an air pump, glass jars, and thermometers, she compared how the temperature inside the jars changed when they were filled with dry air, moist air, carbon dioxide (CO_2), or hydrogen and placed in the sunlight.

HEATING AND COOLING

Her research showed that trapped carbon dioxide gas caused the temperature to rise the most. Eunice wrote, "The receiver containing this gas became itself much heated—very sensibly more so than the other—and on being removed [from sunlight] it was many times as long in cooling." She also found that the heating effect of moist air was greater than that of dry air and concluded, "An atmosphere of that gas [CO_2] would give to our Earth a high temperature."

GREENHOUSE GAS AND CLIMATE

Eunice's paper, "Circumstances Affecting the Heat of the Sun's Rays," was summarized in several journals. Unfortunately, most of them ignored her conclusion that gases we now call "greenhouse gases," such as carbon dioxide, can impact Earth's climate. Her research on sunlight, trapped gases, and water vapor was groundbreaking. Although she was the first person to propose a connection between carbon dioxide and climate change, she wasn't recognized for this accomplishment until 2010, when a geologist named Ray Sorenson came across her work in an old journal.

AN INVENTOR

Eunice Newton Foote continued to study gases and later published a paper on atmospheric pressure and electrical charges. In addition to scientific research, she invented things with her husband. Their inventions included a new type of paper-making machine and a squeakless sole for shoes, made from a single piece of rubber.

IN TODAY'S WORLD

The buildup of greenhouse gases in Earth's atmosphere from human activities such as burning fossil fuel has dramatically warmed our planet and is one of the biggest challenges we face today.

TRY THIS AT HOME!

Make a list of ways you can reduce the amount of carbon dioxide released into the atmosphere by burning fossil fuels. For example, turning off lights, carpooling, walking, and biking can all reduce your "carbon footprint."

Fanny Hesse

AGAR GROWTH MEDIAN

'LINA

Fanny Angelina Eilshemius's friends called her "'Lina." The oldest of ten children, she was born in New York in the summer of 1850 to wealthy Dutch immigrants. There were no vaccines to prevent childhood diseases back then, and five of her siblings died when they were very young. Growing up, she learned to cook from her mother and their servants. When she was fifteen years old, Fanny was sent off to boarding school in Switzerland to study French and economics.

A PARTNER

Fanny met her husband Walther Hesse when he was visiting New York during a stint as a surgeon for a German passenger ship. They met again when her family was in Europe and became engaged. She moved to Germany in 1874 to marry him and was first exposed to science in 1884 when Walther went to work in the lab of the famous microbiologist Robert Koch.

AN ARTIST

From a family of artists, Fanny proved herself to be talented at documenting Walther's research by making colorful medical illustrations of the bacteria he studied. To create accurate drawings of individual bacteria they saw under the microscope, and clumps of bacteria called colonies that could be seen with the naked eye, she had to learn about microbiology.

A LAB ASSISTANT

Besides educating and caring for their three sons, Fanny was Walther's lab assistant. She prepared food called culture medium for the bacteria they were studying. At that time, Robert Koch, Walther, and other microbiologists were having difficulty growing individual colonies of bacteria, which severely limited their research. They mixed nutrients with gelatin to make a flat, bouncy surface where colonies grew well, but on hot days the mixture melted. Certain types of bacteria also made chemicals called enzymes, which could liquify the gelatin.

AGAR

Fanny Hesse had learned when she was young that a substance called agar-agar, or agar, made from red algae, could be added to jelly and pudding to make them resistant to melting. She had the idea to add agar to microbial culture medium and found that it created a long-lasting, heat- and enzyme-resistant surface for growing bacteria. Following her discovery, Robert Koch used Frannie's new agar culture medium recipe in his lab to grow bacteria and went on to make many great discoveries in microbiology. Sadly, Koch never gave Fanny or Walther Hesse credit for their contributions and they never profited from her brilliant idea.

IN TODAY'S WORLD

Agar growth medium is still used in labs around the world every day, in everything from molecular biology research to diagnosing strep throat in clinical labs.

TRY THIS AT HOME!

Make two identical desserts, one with gelatin and one with agar. Test a spoonful of each to see which one melts more easily in hot water and then eat the rest.

Agnes Pockels

SURFACE TENSION

KITCHEN SINK CHEMIST

Agnes Pockels was born in Venice, Italy, in 1862. Her father was an officer in the royal Austrian army, but when she was nine years old, he became very ill with malaria. Her family moved to Brunswick in Lower Saxony, which is part of Germany. Although she attended a high school for girls and was fascinated by science, women were not accepted into universities. Agnes wanted nothing more than to continue her studies, but she was forced to remain at home to take care of her two ailing parents while her brother went off to college.

KITCHEN SINK SCIENCE

Fortunately for the field of chemistry, Agnes's curiosity was unstoppable. She began to notice interesting phenomena while washing dishes in her kitchen sink. Fascinated by how oils and particles formed films on water, she observed that those films could be disturbed by soaps and other materials. Agnes transformed her kitchen into a research station and dove into the study of surface tension, which is the name for the way molecules stick together on the surface of a fluid. Her brother Fredrich, who was studying science at the university, recognized his sister's hunger for knowledge and supported her in every way he could. Besides observing her work, he gave her access to a physics journal so that she could learn what other scientists were doing in their more well-equipped laboratories.

SLIDE TROUGH

By the time she was twenty, Agnes had invented a "slide trough," which allowed her to play with the way a liquid's surface behaved, by sliding a wire or metal strip across the top of it. She used her apparatus to create very thin layers of fluids and then to test the effect of different contaminants, such as fine powders, on surface tension. Besides discovering methods for applying uniform layers of particles to a surface, she discovered that her trough could sweep a surface free of surface contaminants.

PUBLICATION

Agnes shared her results by writing a letter to another scientist who studied the surface of liquids. He was impressed, and eventually her work was published in the famous journal *Nature*. She was delighted to learn that other scientists were using her research results and trough design in their own laboratories. Pockels continue studying surface tension, and her work led to many discoveries and innovations in surface tension research and material science.

A KIND HEART

Agnes Pockels's brother died in 1913, and following World War I her beloved physics journal was no longer published. She lived out the rest of her life in relative obscurity, always helping others. Four years before her death, Agnes was awarded the Laura R. Leonard Prize of the German Colloid Society, "for her quantitative investigation of the properties of interfaces and surface films, and for the methods she used, which have since become fundamental in modern colloid science."

IN TODAY'S WORLD

A small amount of detergent is added to toothpaste to reduce the surface tension of the mixture. This allows the active ingredients, such as fluoride, to spread across teeth during brushing.

TRY THIS AT HOME!

Cover the bottom of a dinner plate with milk and add a few drops of food coloring to the milk without stirring. Add a drop of dish soap to the milk to break the surface tension of the liquid.

Marie Curie
ELEMENTAL EXTRACTION

RADIOACTIVITY PIONEER

Marie Curie, born Manya Sklodowska, entered the world in 1867 surrounded by a loving family in a house filled with laughter, books, and her father's scientific equipment. Although her childhood in Poland was filled with magical moments, challenges loomed from the start. Their lives were overshadowed by an oppressive Russian regime, which forced her father out of his academic job and the family into an apartment where they opened a boarding school to pay the bills. One of the boys who arrived to live with the family carried typhus fever, which killed Marie's beloved sister Zosia. Two years later, tuberculosis took her mother's life.

POLAND

The serious, gray-eyed girl took refuge in her education. By the time she was seventeen, she was actively involved in a secret "floating university," where she began to learn about chemistry and biology and dove into literature and culture. She came to believe that education was the only way to fight oppression. When she went to work as a nanny for a wealthy family, she continued to tutor the poor neighbor children, teaching them to read. Eventually she earned enough money to join her sister in Paris in 1891 to pursue her dream of attending the famous Sorbonne University.

PARIS

Marie fell in love with math and physics and soon graduated at the top of her class at the Sorbonne, despite being so preoccupied with her studies that she often forgot to eat. While searching for a home for some laboratory equipment, she met Pierre Curie, the man who would become her partner in science and in life. Together they embarked on an extraordinary adventure.

STRANGE RAYS

While pursuing her doctorate degree, Marie decided to study the strange new rays that a scientist named Becquerel had discovered emanating from the element uranium. Searching for other elements and minerals naturally emitting these rays, she discovered that uranium mining waste called pitchblende gave a stronger signal than uranium did on its own. By chemically separating the mining waste, she discovered two new elements: polonium and radium.

It took her four years to purify a sample of radium smaller than a grain of rice, but it was worth it when her treasured element took its place on the periodic table and she coined the word "radioactive." She could have made a small fortune by patenting her extraction method, but Marie believed that everyone should benefit from scientific discovery, so she freely shared her technique with the scientific community and industry.

TWO NOBEL PRIZES

Marie Curie went on to become the first woman to win a Nobel Prize in Physics, and later she went on to win a second Nobel in chemistry. Her curiosity, hard work, and determination changed the world, and although radioactivity from her work shortened her life, she continues to inspire scientists today.

IN TODAY'S WORLD

Marie Curie helped to create the first radiation therapy to target and kill cancer cells. Although radium is no longer used for radiation therapy, the technique is still used today to treat certain cancers.

TRY THIS AT HOME!

Most radioactive materials are considered too dangerous to have in homes, but you can learn about them online. Look up some images of radium, one of the elements discovered by Marie Curie.

Susan La Flesche Picotte

PUBLIC HEALTH/HOUSEFLIES

DAUGHTER OF A CHIEF

Susan La Flesche Picotte was born in June of 1865. She was the daughter of Joseph La Flesche, who had been made chief of the Omaha tribe of Nebraska in 1853. Following years of violence and displacement by European settlers, their people divided into those who followed the traditional ways and those, like her father, who believed that the only way to survive was to incorporate the ways of the white man.

She grew up in a log cabin with her three sisters and was sent to a boarding school on the reservation where indigenous students were forced to learn about European and American culture. By the time she went off to college, Susan was fluent in English and French as well as Omaha, which she spoke with her parents.

A LIFE-CHANGING EXPERIENCE

When Susan was eight years old, she watched an elderly woman on the reservation die in pain while waiting for a white doctor. They called the doctor four times, but he never arrived. Later, she recalled thinking, "It was only an Indian, and it did not matter (to him)." Perhaps this motivated her to eventually attend medical school at the Women's Medical College of Pennsylvania, the first medical school in the United States dedicated to educating women to be physicians. Susan took biology, chemistry, anatomy, and physiology classes, and she graduated as the valedictorian of her class.

HOMECOMING

Dr. Picotte returned home to Nebraska to find patients lining up at her door suffering from diseases that included tuberculosis and cholera. She worked twenty-hour days, traveling on miles by foot, horseback, or carriage to help people. After getting married and having two sons, she continued her work, which was unusual for a woman at that time. To control diseases on the reservation, she encouraged good hygiene (cleanliness to improve human health), including fresh air and screen doors to keep disease-carrying flies out of buildings.

"DR. SUSAN"

During her medical career, Susan La Flesche Picotte served more than 1,300 patients spread out over 450 square miles. She became known as "Dr. Susan" and became a local leader. Following the death of her husband, she worked as a defender of the ancestral land belonging to the Omaha tribe and raised enough money to build a hospital on the reservation. She died in 1915.

IN TODAY'S WORLD

Public health experts today understand much more about how disease is spread than they did in Susan La Flesche Picotte's time, but they are still working to find better ways to slow or stop the spread of diseases carried by flies and mosquitoes.

TRY THIS AT HOME!

Make a model of a housefly from Play-Doh with cotton swab legs. Touch the fly's feet to an ink stamp pad and then onto paper to see how flies pick up germs and spread them around.

Mary Agnes Chase

AGROSTOLOGY/GRASSES

DAUGHTER OF A BLACKSMITH
In 1869, Mary Agnes Meara was born in Iroquois County in Illinois. Mary's father was a railroad blacksmith and her family changed their last name to Merrill to avoid the prejudice faced by working-class Irish immigrants. He died when she was only two years old and her family moved to Chicago. Mary's family was poor, so when she finished grade school, she had to go to work at the newspaper to support them and wasn't able to continue her formal education.

THE EXPOSITION
When she was only nineteen, Mary married a man in the newspaper business and changed her name to Mary Agnes Chase, but her husband died of tuberculosis a year later. In 1893, Mary and her nephew attended Chicago's Columbian Exposition, which was a huge fair, and saw an exhibit about plants. Mary was so fascinated by what she learned there that she decided to study botany.

A TALENTED ARTIST
Mary started her own field journals about plants and one of her professors was so impressed with her drawings that she was hired to illustrate books. She learned to use a microscope and worked as a meat inspector at the Chicago stockyards before returning to work with plants at the Chicago Field Museum. Eventually, she got a job with the United States Department of Agriculture, where she worked her way up from illustrator to lab assistant to principal scientist in charge of agrostology, the study of grasses. She traveled the world collecting more than 20,000 species of grasses and was the first to document several of them.

A HUMAN RIGHTS ADVOCATE
Throughout her career, Mary Agnes Chase worked tirelessly to make science accessible and understandable to everyone. Sometimes, she risked her career to speak up for human rights. In addition to mentoring underprivileged students, including women who wanted to be botanists, she was a suffragist who was arrested twice, protesting for women's right to vote.

A COLLEGE DEGREE
In her long career, Mary Agnes Chase published more than seventy articles and books, including a popular guide to grasses for nonprofessionals, called *Agnes Chases's First Book of Grasses*, which is still in print. When she was eighty-nine years old, she finally received her first college degree, an honorary degree from the University of Illinois.

IN TODAY'S WORLD
The study of agrostology is still important today. Crop plants such as rice, corn, wheat, and sugarcane are all grasses. Healthy grasslands prevent soil erosion and help with the problem of climate change by soaking up carbon dioxide from the air.

TRY THIS AT HOME!
Fold a paper towel, get it wet, and slide it into a small plastic sandwich bag so it is flat. Sprinkle grass seeds across the surface of the paper towel. Tape the bag in a sunny window and keep the paper towel damp. Watch the grass seeds germinate (sprout).

Ynés Mexía

PLANT COLLECTION/IDENTIFICATION

NATURE-LOVER

Ynés Enriquetta Juliette Mexía was born in 1870 in Washington D.C. Her father was a Mexican diplomat, and when her parents divorced, she moved to Texas with her mother. No matter where she was, whether it was Texas or Mexico, she loved taking long walks and studying the birds and plants she encountered. As a young woman, Ynés couldn't attend college, but even as an adult, she remained interested in the natural world.

CALIFORNIA

In 1909, Ynés moved to San Francisco, California. After experiencing personal tragedies, she was mentally and physically exhausted, but she found comfort in the beautiful mountains and redwood trees of Northern California. She became an active member of the Sierra Club, and signed up for a botany course at the University of California–Berkeley.

SLEEPING UNDER THE STARS

Ynés was fifty-one when she started taking classes at Berkeley, and she went on her first major plant-collecting expeditions to in 1925, when she was fifty-five. Ignoring the male explorers who said that it would be impossible for a woman to travel alone in South America, she continued taking trips up and down the Americas, wearing pants, riding horses, and sleeping under the stars. She survived an earthquake, poisonous berries, and extremely difficult conditions on her quest to discover new species and document especially interesting plants, such as the wax palm tree, which could grow up to 200 feet (61 m) tall. Ynés Mexía joined other expeditions as well, including one to Brazil headed by Agnes Chase and her colleague A. S. Hitchcock. Her assistant, Nina Floy Bracelin, prepared and helped identify the plants Ynés collected.

A SCIENCE COMMUNICATOR

Although Ynés Mexía was so busy collecting plants that she never finished her college degree, she gathered almost 150,000 species. In thirteen short years, Ynés discovered 500 new plant species and 2 new genera. Between expeditions, she gave lectures in San Francisco, shared photographs of her journeys, and taught people about plants. Ynés suffered from prejudice because of her Mexican heritage, her age, and her gender, but everyone who knew her said that she was friendly, unassuming, and tough. She died in 1938 in Berkeley, California.

IN TODAY'S WORLD

Today, specimens collected by Ynés Mexía can be found in museums from New York to San Francisco.

TRY THIS AT HOME!

Collect plants and flowers and try to identify them using a book or an app. Place the plants between pieces of newspaper sandwiched between thicker pieces of paper and press them with a heavy book or another flat, heavy object until they are dry.

Lise Meitner

NUCLEAR FISSION

VIENNA

Lise Meitner was born in 1878 in Vienna, a large city that was then in the multinational state of Austria-Hungary. The third of eight children, she had four sisters and three brothers. Lise's family was Jewish, and her father was a lawyer. Although they valued education, at that time girls were not allowed to pursue an education beyond primary (grade) school. When Lise was eight years old, she kept a notebook of her observations. She wrote about the rainbow of colors she saw in a thin film of oil and about the reflection of light. It was the beginning of her love of science and math.

A TOUGH EXAM

In 1901, women were finally allowed to take an entrance exam at the University of Vienna. Cramming the eight years of education she had missed into two years, Lise was one of few women admitted to the school. In college, she developed an interest in physics and became the second woman to earn a doctoral degree at the university.

ATOMIC WOMAN

A talented researcher, Dr. Meitner studied radioactivity. Some of her experiments involved sending beams of radioactive particles into metal foil, such as aluminum foil. She was surprised to find that the higher the atomic mass of the metal in the foil was, the more the radioactive particles scattered when they hit it. Her work later helped a man named Ernest Rutherford determine the structure of atoms.

A COLLEAGUE

Lise Meitner moved to Berlin, Germany, which was called Prussia back then. She attended lectures by the famous physicist Max Planck and did research with a scientist named Otto Hahn. Women were not allowed at the research institute where she worked, so she had to work in a woodshop, which served as her laboratory, and use the bathroom at a restaurant down the street. Otto Hahn was made a professor, but Meitner was not paid for her work. After a few years, things got better. She became friends with several physicists at the institute, but she was never paid as well as Otto.

AN ESCAPE

As an adult, Lise converted to the Christian religion, but World War II put her in grave danger because of her Jewish heritage. Otto Hahn helped her escape to Sweden, where she was safe. Sadly, all her equipment was in Germany, and she could not continue her research in person. Hahn continued to send her his experimental results, which suggested that the nucleus of an element called uranium could be split.

A REVELATION

Although Hahn could not decipher how a nucleus could split apart, Lise figured it out. While walking through wintery Swedish woods with her nephew, she imagined a droplet of water splitting in half—like a dividing cell. Lise pulled out a piece of paper and did the mathematical calculations. They added up. She wrote to Hahn and they both published papers on the phenomenon, which Meitner called fission. Otto Hahn was awarded a Nobel Prize for their discovery, but Lise Meitner was left out and got nothing. Eventually she won many other prizes for her work. Dr. Meitner hoped that her discovery would be used for good, rather than for destruction.

IN TODAY'S WORLD

Nuclear reactors use uranium as fuel to create controlled fission reactions that produce energy without burning fossil fuels.

TRY THIS AT HOME!

Roll Play-Doh into a ball to represent the nucleus of an atom undergoing nuclear fission, which means splitting in two. Sculpt the ball into an elongated egg shape. Pinch the center of the cylinder and roll each half into a new ball. As you separate the halves, imagine an enormous amount of energy being released.

Alice Ball

ORGANIC SEPARATION

FAMILY OF ARTISTS

Born in 1892 in Seattle, Alice Ball was exposed to chemistry at a very young age. Her grandfather was a famous photographer and one of the first people in the United States to take daguerreotype images, which required the use of iodine, copper, and mercury. Sadly, her grandfather was ill, possibly as a result of chemical exposure, and Alice's family moved to Hawaii for a year in hopes that the sunny climate and sea air would improve his health. When he died, they returned to Seattle, where Alice received degrees in pharmaceutical chemistry and pharmacy from the University of Washington.

HAWAII

For graduate school, Alice chose to attend the University of Hawaii, where she became the first woman and the first African American to earn a master's degree in chemistry at the school. For her graduate thesis, Alice separated out the chemical parts of kava root, in order to discover its active components. Harry Hollman, an assistant surgeon at a nearby hospital, heard about her work on kava root and asked her to help solve the problem of treating Hansen's disease, which is also called leprosy. A leper colony had been established on the Hawaiian island of Molokai in 1865, and thousands of Hawaiians with the disease had been sent there in an attempt to stop the spread of the disease.

A NEW TREATMENT FOR LEPROSY

As a professor at the University of Hawaii, Ball devoted every moment that she wasn't teaching to synthesizing a better treatment for the disfiguring disease. At the time, the only way to reduce the symptoms of Hansen's disease was to inject or swallow chaulmoogra oil, which had been extracted from the seeds of a type of evergreen tree. Unfortunately, the oil didn't work well. Painful injections formed a necklace of blisters under the skin that weren't easily absorbed by the patient's bodies, and the oil tasted so horrible it was impossible to drink without vomiting. In only a year, twenty-three-year-old Professor Ball figured out how to separate the oil into parts until she found a compound that could be extracted and made into an easily absorbable medicine for victims of Hansen's disease.

STOLEN WORK

Tragically, Alice Ball died when she was only twenty-four years old, soon after making her discovery. She may have died from exposure to chlorine gas during a lab demonstration, but it is unclear. Her death certificate was altered to state that she died of tuberculosis. The university's president, who was also a chemist, took over Ball's studies, publishing her results under his own name, and producing large quantities of the medicine she'd created.

AN ALLY

When he realized what had happened, Harry Hollman made it public that credit for Alice Ball's discovery had been stolen by the president of the university. Hollman published a paper of his own, crediting Alice for her work and dubbing her leprosy treatment the "Ball Method." Until effective antibiotics were invented in the 1940s, Alice Ball's treatment was the only effective medicine for Hansen's disease.

IN TODAY'S WORLD

Recently the University of Hawaii erected a plaque in her honor, awarded her a medal, and named a scholarship after her. The state of Hawaii now celebrates "Alice Ball Day." Organic separations processes similar to the methods used by Dr. Ball are still used in the pharmaceutical industry today.

TRY THIS AT HOME!

Use a garlic press to squeeze organic compounds from a chopped orange or lemon peels. Collect the oil floating on top of the juice and use it to flavor food or add scent to homemade soap or candles.

Gerty Cori

THE CORI CYCLE

SETTING SAIL

Named after a transatlantic ship, Gerty Theresa Cori was born in Prague in 1896. Her father was a chemist who directed a sugar refinery, and she was tutored at home by her mother until she was ten and began attending the local school for girls. By the time she was sixteen, Gerty had decided that she wanted to be a medical doctor but discovered that she lacked many of the classes that were required. She worked extremely hard and over a year learned the science, language, and math she would need to study medicine. Her uncle, who was a professor of pediatrics, encouraged her to apply to medical school and she was admitted to a university in Prague.

A LAB PARTNER

While she was in medical school, Gerty met Carl Cori, who thought that she was smart and funny. They both loved the outdoors and working in a laboratory. After finishing medical school, they married and Gerty went to work in a laboratory at a children's hospital, where she did research on thyroid disease in children. In 1922, they moved to the United States, where they hoped Gerty wouldn't be discriminated against on the basis of her Jewish heritage. They became U.S. citizens and went to work together at what is now the Roswell Park Comprehensive Cancer Center in New York.

THE CORI CYCLE

A director at the Roswell Research Institute, who didn't like having women in the laboratory, tried his best to get rid of Gerty, but Carl stood up for her and she refused to leave. Despite the hostile environment, the Coris worked together day and night to study how the human body turns carbohydrates into energy. In 1929, they proposed a "cycle of carbohydrates" in which a sugar called glucose in muscles is cleaved into lactic acid, which the liver can turn back into glucose for muscles to utilize again. Gerty was listed as the first author on the papers related to this work, and today that cycle is named after her and Carl. Eventually, the Coris moved to Washington University in St. Louis, where they continued their research. Gerty returned to her love of pediatric medicine by studying metabolic disorders in children.

A NOBEL PRIZE

In 1945 Gerty Cori became the first American woman, and the third woman ever, to win a Nobel Prize in science when she and Carl were awarded the Nobel Prize for Physiology or Medicine for their work on the Cori cycle. Sadly, like Marie Curie and Irene Curie who also won Nobel prizes, Dr. Cori's early death was probably the result of radiation exposure. Her contributions to science are foundational to scientific research that continues today.

IN TODAY'S WORLD

Dr. Cori's work on the Cori cycle is important for modern research on a disease called diabetes. Diabetes is a treatable disease that affects many people, and scientists are working hard to find a cure.

TRY THIS AT HOME!

Line up three clear jars or glasses. Label the end jars "muscle" and the center jar "liver." Fold and trim two paper towels to form bridges between the jars, reaching to the bottom. Fill one end jar with water and add a few drops of food coloring. The water will move from jar to jar via capillary action, representing how the body moves lactic acid waste from muscles to the liver, where it is turned into a sugar called glucose and then returned to muscles.

Katharine Burr Blodgett

THIN FILMS

PHYSICS

LEARNING FRENCH

Katharine Burr Blodgett was born in 1898. Katharine's father, a patent attorney in Schenectady, New York, was shot to death during a robbery shortly before her birth. Her mother moved with Katherine and her brother to Paris, France, when they were young, so they could learn a second language.

SCHOOL IN AMERICA

After going back and forth between New York and Europe for several years, Katharine finally started school when she was eight years old. She did well at her studies and got a scholarship to Bryn Mawr College, where she was inspired by her math professor Charlotte Angas Scott and her physics professor James Barnes. After college, she went to the University of Chicago to get her master's degree. While she was there, Katharine studied gas masks to learn how different materials absorbed (attached to) gases.

GENERAL ELECTRIC

Katharine went to work at General Electric, where she worked in the lab of Irving Langmuir for six years before going to Cambridge University in England to get her doctoral degree. One of very few women at Cambridge, she studied with the famous physicist Ernest Rutherford and became the first woman to earn a doctoral degree in physics from the university.

THIN FILMS

Returning to General Electric, Dr. Katharine Blodgett resumed the work she had been doing with Irving Langmuir. Interested in designing techniques for applying thin films of fluids on surfaces such as glass and metal, she refined a piece of equipment called the Langmuir-Blodgett trough. The pan-like apparatus* allowed her to float oily substances on water, and she used them to coat glass and metal. Some of the layers she created were a single molecule thick.

INVISIBLE GLASS

By adding layer after layer of non-reflective coating to glass until she had forty-four thin layers, Katharine created glass with no reflection, which proved extremely useful. Her non-reflective glass was used for movie cameras, telescopes, non-reflective eyeglasses, and submarine periscopes and spy cameras during World War II.

A CREATIVE MIND

Katharine Burr Blodgett won many awards and was inducted into the National Inventors Hall of Fame. Besides non-reflective glass, she invented a "color ruler" that allowed scientists to measure the thickness of thin layers and a device to measure humidity. Katharine was a conservationist and an actress in her local theater, and she loved gardening. She also liked playing cards, writing funny poetry, and looking through telescopes. Dr. Burr Blodgett died in 1979.

IN TODAY'S WORLD

Katharine Burr Blodget's thin-film technique, which creates Langmuir-Blodgett (LB) films, is used to make computer components and anti-reflective glass, among other things.

*The design of the Langmuir-Blodgett (LB) trough was inspired by an apparatus designed by Agnes Pockels (pages 20–21).

TRY THIS AT HOME!

Fill a disposable flat container with water. Cut black paper into pieces smaller than the container. Add a drop of clear nail polish to water. Wearing gloves, quickly lay the paper on the water. Try to lift the clear, thin film of nail polish floating on the water. It may take a few tries.

Cecilia Payne-Gaposchkin

STAR MATERIAL

A LIBRARY

Cecilia Payne was born in Buckinghamshire, England in 1900. Her father died when she was only four, leaving her mother to raise Cecilia and her two siblings. The family was financially well-off and had a large library, where Cecilia read literature and learned about music and theater. They moved to London when she was twelve, so her brother could go to a better school.

AN EDUCATION

Cecilia's talent for music led the well-known composer Gustav Holst to encourage her to make a career of it. She loved science more than music, though, and she won a scholarship to Newnham College, a women's college at Cambridge University. At that time, few women studied science and they had to sit at the front of lecture halls, enduring the teasing of male students. Cecilia kept her focus and completed her studies there, although at the time, Cambridge did not award degrees to women.

STARS IN HER EYES

Cecilia became fascinated with the stars while attending a lecture by a man named Arthur Eddington. He spoke about photographing stars off the coast of Africa in 1919 during a total eclipse of the sun to test Albert Einstein's theory of relativity. She was so excited about his lecture that she almost had a nervous breakdown.

STELLAR RESEARCH

In 1923, Cecilia moved to the United States to work with the astronomer Harlow Shapley at the Harvard Observatory. She spent the next two years working day and night to analyze thousands of images from the observatory's collection of stellar spectra, which contained the light signatures from stars. Cecilia combined the data she interpreted from the collection with a new theory developed by Meghnad Saha, a scientist from India, and came up with a revolutionary theory of her own—that the sun is made mostly of hydrogen and that helium is the second most plentiful element.

A BRILLIANT THESIS

When Cecilia showed her work to Harlow Shapley and his colleague Henry Norris Russell, they rejected her conclusion, siding with the current theory that the sun had the same elemental composition as Earth. She published her thesis, but downplayed her discovery, and became the first woman to earn a doctoral degree in astronomy from Harvard. It was not until Russell came to the same conclusion himself years later that people accepted that the sun was made of hydrogen and helium. Russell was congratulated for "his" discovery, while Cecilia got no credit until decades later.

A TRAILBLAZER

Dr. Cecilia Payne married a Russian astronomer named Sergei Gaposchkin and they had three children who spent many hours in the observatory because Harvard didn't pay them enough to afford childcare. In 1956, Cecilia became the first female professor of the Harvard Faculty in Arts and Sciences and the first woman to head a department there. Besides writing five books, she has an asteroid named for her.

IN TODAY'S WORLD

Every object reflects, absorbs, or produces light waves. Spectroscopy is a technique that uses a prism or grooves to split light waves from an object, such as a star, into its different wavelengths. It is one of the most powerful tools used by astronomers today to study what stars are made of.

TRY THIS AT HOME!

Use the grooved side of a compact disc to focus sunlight onto a piece of white paper and create a rainbow. This collection of colors is called a spectrum. Spectrums are like fingerprints and the wavelength of the colors tells scientists what elements celestial objects are made of.

Dora Priaulx Henry

BARNACLES

A BIG MOVE

Dora Priaulx was born in Maquoketa, Iowa, in 1904. Both of her parents were teachers. After the death of her father, when she was five, her mother moved Dora and her brothers to Los Angeles. School came easily to Dora and she graduated from Hollywood High School before getting a biology degree from the University of California at Berkeley, where she married a fellow student named Bernard Henry.

FROM PARASITES TO BARNACLES

After completing her PhD in parasitology at UC Berkeley, Dora and Bernard moved to Seattle, where she began to study parasites called gregarines, which were infecting barnacles in Puget Sound. As she worked, her interest shifted from the parasites to the barnacles themselves. She started collecting barnacles, identifying them and writing papers about the fascinating invertebrates, which attach headfirst to boats, rocks, whales, crustaceans, and almost anything else in the water.

WORLD WAR II

The Smithsonian Institution in Washington, D.C., was impressed by Dora's expansive knowledge and encouraged her to study their museum barnacle collections. She was also an important consultant for Ed Ricketts in his early work on intertidal ecology and is mentioned in *The Log from the Sea of Cortez*, which he wrote with the famous author John Steinbeck. Barnacle growth can present a big problem for ships, and World War II led Dora to work as an assistant oceanographer with the air force and then to the navy's Hydrographic Office.

TRAVEL ABROAD

Interested in the distribution patterns of barnacles, Dora was the first to accurately plot the range of places where they grew, on a map. She continued to study barnacles until she was ninety-three years old. Her fieldwork took her from Lower California and the Gulf of California to the Gulf of Mexico, the Central Pacific Islands, and Bermuda. She discovered new species, learned new things about barnacle reproduction, and wrote countless papers.

AN EDUCATOR

Dr. Dora Priaulx Henry loved to travel. In 1968, she helped develop a "Coasts of the World" travel course, which took students and faculty to the South Pacific and South America to learn about wind, waves, tides, volcanoes, glaciers, beaches, and life in the intertidal and near-shore environments. She always welcomed visits from colleagues from around the world. Today, her barnacle collection can be found at the Smithsonian Institution's Museum of Natural History.

IN TODAY'S WORLD

Barnacles still present a challenge to boats, but researchers are very interested in the strong glue they make to cement themselves to wet objects very quickly. One group of researchers has copied their oily adhesive to make a substance that can be applied to wounds to quickly stop bleeding.

TRY THIS AT HOME!

Tie several short pieces of yarn to the end of a stick to represent barnacle legs. On the bottom of a paper cup, draw two long curved lines on opposite sides. Connect them in the center to create what looks like the letter "I" with curved serifs. Cut along the lines to make a flapped door, representing the calcium plates on barnacles. Push your barnacle legs up and down through the door to show how barnacles emerge to feed and retreat from predators.

Maria Goeppert-Mayer

NUCLEAR SHELL MODEL

AN EDUCATION

Atoms are the building blocks of matter. Maria Goeppert-Mayer is best known for discovering how the spinning of protons and neutrons inside of atoms affects the structure of the nucleus and the stability of different elements. Born in 1906, Goeppert-Mayer grew up in Germany admiring her father, a sixth-generation professor of pediatrics who understood the importance of educating women. Although the preparatory school for girls she attended closed, Maria and four other girls continued to study and were able to pass their exams for acceptance into the university.

JUMPING ELECTRONS

Germany needed teachers for girls' schools and Maria Goeppert had planned to study math in college, but she found herself irresistibly drawn to physics and pursued a PhD in that discipline. In her doctoral paper, she described a theory called two-photon absorption that correctly predicted that bundles of energy called photons can make electrons jump to higher energy levels.

COMING TO AMERICA

In 1930, Goeppert married another scientist named Joseph Mayer. They moved to Baltimore, Maryland, in the United States, where Joseph had been offered a job at Johns Hopkins University. Maria was not offered a job, because there was an outdated rule against hiring spouses, which had become an excuse not to hire women as professors. They gave her a job writing letters in German, and in return she got a tiny salary along with access to a lab where she could continue her research. She also got to teach a few classes but was not paid.

PHYSICS "FOR THE FUN OF IT"

In 1937, Joseph went to work at Columbia University and Maria was given an office but no salary. She continued her research for the sheer pleasure of doing physics.

MANHATTAN TO CHICAGO

Shortly after beginning her first paid teaching position at Sarah Lawrence College, Dr. Goeppert-Mayer was recruited to work on the Manhattan Project, which eventually produced the world's first atomic bombs and brought World War II to an end. She and Joseph moved to Chicago, where she was offered a part-time job as a senior physicist at the nearby Argonne National Laboratory.

A WALTZ

It was in Chicago that Goeppert-Meyer did her Noble Prize–winning research on the structure of the nuclei of atoms. She liked to describe nuclei as concentric circles of waltzing couples, some spinning clockwise and others counterclockwise while the couples twirl "round and round." In 1960 Maria Goeppert-Meyer finally became a full professor. In 1963 she shared a Nobel Prize with J. Hans D. Jensen and Eugene Paul Wigner for her discoveries concerning nuclear shell structure, becoming the second woman in history to win a Nobel Prize in Physics.

IN TODAY'S WORLD

Today, astrophysicists are using the nuclear shell model to understand the science of exploding stars called supernovas.

TRY THIS AT HOME!

Use an orange or a Styrofoam ball to represent the nucleus of an atom. Use materials such as wire, wooden skewers, and beads to make a Bohr model of an element on the periodic table. Each element's atomic number will tell you how many electrons orbit the nucleus, and you can look up their arrangement in a book or online. Protons and neutrons are found inside the nucleus.

Mary Golda Ross

AEROSPACE ENGINEERING

PHYSICS

GREAT GRANDDAUGHTER OF A CHIEF

Mary Golda Ross was born in Park Hill, Oklahoma, in 1908. The second of five children, she was the great granddaughter of John Ross, who had been the chief of the Cherokee nation from 1828 to 1866. Despite the best efforts of Indigenous leaders such as John Ross, the United States government had forcibly removed a hundred thousand Native Americans from their land and resettled them in Oklahoma in a deadly, devastating march from their homes known as "The Trail of Tears."

TAHLEQUAH

Mary was extremely bright, and she was happy to be brought up in the Cherokee tradition of equal education for boys and girls. Her parents sent her to live with her grandparents in Tahlequah, the capital of the Cherokee Nation, which stood beside the foothills of the Ozark Mountains. When she turned sixteen, Mary went to Northeastern State Teachers College in Tahlequah, where she earned her bachelor's degree in mathematics.

THE GREAT DEPRESSION

During the Great Depression, Mary taught math and science at a school out in the countryside. After teaching for nine years, she went to work at the Bureau of Indian Affairs in Washington, D.C. and then at an American Indian boarding school in Santa Fe, New Mexico. In 1938, Mary moved to Colorado to get a master's degree in mathematics. While she was in school there, she took as many astronomy classes as she could.

THE WAR

When World War II broke out, Mary moved to California to work for Lockheed, an American aerospace company. Her job included studying the effects of air pressure on fighter jets and water pressure on submarine-launched vehicles. Mary was so smart and talented that in 1952 she was made part of a top-secret think tank called "skunkworks" in which she was the only woman and the only Native American.

A ROCKET SCIENTIST

After the war, Mary studied aerospace engineering as she continued to work on designing satellites and rockets. She was part of the Space Race, which aimed to send humans out of Earth's orbit. At Lockheed, Mary helped write NASA's Planetary Flight Handbook, a guide to space travel. She believed that women would make great astronauts, although she added "I'd rather stay down here and analyze the data."

AN INSPIRING FIGURE

Mary Golda Ross eventually became a senior advanced systems staff engineer at Lockheed. When she retired, Mary spoke at schools, encouraging young women and Indigenous youths to consider careers in technology and engineering. At the age of ninety-six, she participated in the opening ceremonies for the National Museum of the American Indian in Washington D.C. Her image can be found on the 2019 one-dollar coin, along with that of American Indian astronaut John Herrington, whom her work helped launch into space in 2002.

IN TODAY'S WORLD

The work of Mary Golda Ross and her colleagues is engrained in today's aerospace industry, from rocket designs to satellites.

TRY THIS AT HOME!

Look up instructions on how to fold a paper airplane and test how far it will fly. Then, change the wing and tail design to see whether you can engineer that type of plane to fly farther. Try the same thing with other paper airplane designs.

Rachel Carson

ENVIRONMENTAL CONTAMINANTS

A NATURE LOVER

Rachel Carson always wanted to be a writer and published her first article for a children's magazine when she was eleven. Born in Springdale, Pennsylvania, in 1907, she loved reading and exploring nature. The fields and woods near her house were filled with birds and other animals, although on some days, everything was coated with gray ash from steel mills downriver from where she lived. Her family struggled to pay the bills, and Rachel's mother gave piano lessons to help support Rachel and her two siblings.

AWAKENED BY BIRDS

Every morning, Rachel woke to hear the birds singing. She worked very hard in school, and in her senior paper for high school she wrote that a "thinking, reasoning mind" was a person's most valuable possession. Her parents sold off part of their land to help pay for her college. Rachel got a master's degree from Johns Hopkins University and spent time at the Marine Biological Laboratory in Woods Hole, Massachusetts, where she explored tide pools and fell in love with the sea.

AN AUTHOR

After graduating, Rachel found a job as a writer for the U.S. Department of Fish and Wildlife. Finding inspiration in the natural world, she started to write books about the sea, weaving in geology, chemistry, and biology. With words, she painted beautiful images of the intertidal zones and the open ocean, making science engaging and easy to understand. Rachael organized her descriptions of marine ecosystems by zones that started on shore and moved to deeper water. By 1962, she was a best-selling author.

DDT

Near where Rachel worked in Maryland, a new pesticide (insect killer) called DDT was being tested for safety. Her job at the Department of Fish and Wildlife made her a witness to some of the first reports that DDT was also deadly to fish and wildlife populations. Her background in science helped her understand that DDT could move through soil and water from the fields and wetlands where it had been sprayed into nearby lakes, streams, and rivers. The chemical moved up the food chain, from invertebrates into the bodies of fish, birds, and mammals, often killing them or making it harder for them to reproduce.

AN ACTIVIST FOR NATURE

In 1962, Rachel sparked the environmental movement. She noticed the gradual disappearance of birds after the government started spraying DDT around the United States, and she wrote a book called *Silent Spring*. The book was a best-seller and used scientific evidence to show that DDT was harming ecosystems. The huge corporations that produced DDT called Rachel "hysterical," and "an uninformed woman speaking of that which she did not know." But she refused to be silent and in 1972, the use of DDT was banned in the United States.

IN TODAY'S WORLD

Rachel Carson reminded us that what we do to the environment, we do to ourselves. Many of today's ecologists study the impacts of human behavior on Earth's ecosystems, searching for ways we can maintain healthy relationships with other living things.

* ECOLOGY *

TRY THIS AT HOME!

Dip toothpicks in food coloring, poke them into clear or yellow Jell-O or gelatin and refrigerate for 24 hours. Over time, the dots of food coloring will spread out as the dye moves through the gelatin. This illustrates how chemicals such as pesticides disperse through soil.

Chien-Shiung Wu

SYMMETRY

* PHYSICS *

A SUPPORTIVE FATHER

Born in 1912, Chien-Shiung Wu loved both her parents, but was especially close to her father, who believed that girls should have an education. She and her two brothers grew up in a small fishing village in the Jiangsu province of China. Until she turned eleven and went away to boarding school, Chien attended an elementary school for girls that had been founded by her dad.

A SEA VOYAGE

After graduating at the top of her class, Chien attended National Central University in Nanjing, where she studied math and then physics. She worked in a lab for a few years following graduation and then boarded a ship for America, with plans to attend the University of Michigan for graduate school. After she arrived in San Francisco, a young scientist named Luke Chia-Lu Yuan took her on a tour of the Radiation Laboratory established by Ernest Lawrence in Berkeley.

CHANGE OF PLANS

When Chien heard that women were not allowed to use the front entrance at the University of Michigan, she stayed in Berkeley to pursue her doctoral degree there, in the Radiation Laboratory. Chien used the cyclotron particle accelerator Dr. Lawrence had developed to study a process called beta decay. To do this, she measured electromagnetic energy, called radiation, which was given off by charged particles when they crashed into other particles. In 1940, Chien received her doctoral degree.

THE MANHATTAN PROJECT

Eventually, Dr. Chien-Shiung Wu married Yuan. Chien and Yuan moved to the East Coast, and Dr. Wu taught at Smith College and Princeton, where she was the first woman faculty member of the physics department. During World War II, she joined the Manhattan Project, which was developing the atomic bomb. In addition to improving radiation detection equipment such as Geiger counters, she helped solve a problem that was shutting down an important nuclear reactor. After the war, Dr. Wu became a professor at Columbia University in New York.

THE WU EXPERIMENT

As Dr. Wu continued to study beta decay, she was approached by two of her colleagues who were trying to prove a theory they had about how certain subatomic particles behave. They believed certain symmetrical particles that looked identical, but were mirror images of one another, did not always behave in the same way. The men, Dr. Lee and Dr. Yang, had drawn a rough sketch of an experiment out on paper, but didn't have the expertise to perform it themselves.

Dr. Wu developed a technique that allowed her to perform the experiment using strong magnetic fields, extremely low temperatures, and radioactive cobalt. She demonstrated that under the experimental conditions she had created, Lee and Yang's theory was correct. The famous experiment was named the Wu experiment, but her contribution to the groundbreaking work was ignored when Lee and Yang were awarded the 1957 Nobel Prize.

THE WOLF PRIZE

In addition to the Wu experiment, Dr. Wu confirmed Enrico Fermi's theory of beta decay and studied molecular changes in sickle cell disease. She was awarded the prestigious Wolf Prize in 1978. Dr. Wu is buried in her hometown in China in the courtyard of the school her father established.

IN TODAY'S WORLD

Dr. Chien-Shiung Wu was an activist against gender discrimination and is a role model for women in science.

TRY THIS AT HOME!

Fold a piece of paper in half. Unfold it and paint a name or design on one side of the fold. Refold the paper along the same line, smoothing it to transfer the paint to the other half. Unfold it. You have created a symmetrical image.

Anna Jane Harrison

ORGANIC COMPOUNDS/ULTRAVIOLET LIGHT

ONE-ROOM SCHOOLHOUSE

Anna Jane Harrison grew up on a farm in Missouri. When she asked her father about caterpillars, he taught her about the tractors instead of the butterfly larvae. She tucked the memory away as her earliest brush with science. When he died in 1919, her mother continued running the farm to support seven-year-old Anna and her brother. Anna loved going to school in a one-room schoolhouse and was inspired by her wonderful teacher there.

TEACHING

She attended college and graduate school at the University of Missouri, studying chemistry and education, and she taught at the one-room schoolhouse that she had attended as a child. In 1940, she finished her PhD in physical chemistry. She went to work teaching chemistry at a women's college in New Orleans.

SMOKE DETECTOR

During World War II, Anna took a break from teaching and went to work doing research for the government. In a lab in Kansas City, Missouri, she studied toxic smoke for the National Defense Research Committee and did some work at Corning Glass Works in New York. Some of the work she did resulted in the invention of smoke detectors.

LIGHT WORK

Dr. Harrison joined the faculty at Mount Holyoke College in Massachusetts to work with Emma P. Carr, an expert on ultraviolet spectroscopy, a laboratory technique that uses light waves to analyze chemicals. In addition to using spectroscopy to study chemicals, Harrison used a technique called flash photolysis to break organic chemicals apart.

As the reaction happened, she used spectroscopy to see what chemical fragments were created and whether they interacted with each other. She was especially interested in how organic compounds, which contain carbon linked to other elements, interact with ultraviolet light.

PUBLIC EDUCATION

Anna's students loved her. Besides having a good sense of humor, she was able to communicate complicated concepts in terms that everyone could understand. Dr. Harrison felt that it was essential for the public and policy makers to have a basic understanding of science, so that they could make decisions that would benefit everyone.

TRAVELING FOR SCIENCE

In 1978 Anna Harrison became the first female president of the American Chemical Society, and in 1983 she was named president of the American Association for the Advancement of Science. Her work gave her the opportunity to travel around the world on a mission to improve the way scientists talk to each other and communicate with the public. Dr. Harrison died in Massachusetts in 1998 when she was eighty-five years old.

IN TODAY'S WORLD

Today, organic photochemistry makes it easier for chemists to produce complex organic molecules for industry and research.

TRY THIS AT HOME!

On a baking sheet, arrange a stencil or some leaves on a piece of inexpensive, colorful construction paper. Cover with plastic wrap, weigh the wrap down with rocks, and place it in direct sunlight for several hours. Remove the plastic wrap and leaves or stencil to see how the chemicals in the paper fade in the Sun's ultraviolet light.

Ruby Payne-Scott

SUNSPOTS

A WELL-ROUNDED STUDENT

Ruby Payne-Scott was born in 1912 in New South Wales, a state on the east coast of Australia. As a child, Ruby moved to Sydney to live with her aunt. She attended grade school and high school there, winning honors in both math and biology. At the University of Sydney, she studied physics, chemistry, mathematics, and botany, graduating with a master's degree in physics in 1936.

MAGNETS AND CHICKENS

Ruby worked at a laboratory at the university for a while, studying the effect of strong magnets on developing chicks. She left to teach high school for a few years before eventually landing a job as a librarian at an electronics company that made and operated radios. They discovered her talent for research, and soon Ruby began taking measurements and doing electrical engineering.

TOP SECRET

During World War II, Ruby joined Australia's Radiophysics Laboratory, where she did top-secret work on radar technology. Before long, Ruby Payne-Scott was Australia's top expert on the radar used to detect enemy aircraft. After the war, she continued to improve radar systems and led the laboratory in a new direction—using radar to examine scientific questions.

NOISY SUNSPOTS

In 1946, the science journal *Nature* published a letter from Ruby showing a correlation between sunspots (bright flares on the sun's surface) and increased electromagnetic radio wave emissions from the sun. She and her colleagues took radio wave measurements from seaside cliff tops that confirmed her theory that sunspots produce radio bursts. Ruby designed a piece of equipment called a swept-lobe interferometer, which scanned the sky, picking up radio signals. This allowed radio astronomers to focus in on certain radio signatures that interested them.

A SECRET WEDDING

Ruby married a man named Bill Hall in 1944, but the wedding was kept secret because married women were not allowed to hold public-service jobs such as hers. When the marriage was discovered, Ruby fought to keep her job. She was fired from her permanent position, although she was permitted to keep working without a job title. When she had children, Ruby was forced to quit work entirely, because there was no maternity leave.

A CAT LOVER

When her son and daughter were older, Ruby Payne-Scott returned to radio astronomy and teaching. Besides science and her family, Ruby loved cats. She also enjoyed walking in the Australian outback and knitting. She died in 1981.

IN TODAY'S WORLD

Ruby's work in radioastronomy helped create the technology used to discover black holes and pulsars. It also helped scientists understand the effect of solar storms on electrical systems on Earth.

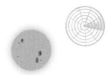

TRY THIS AT HOME!

Build a solar viewer by cutting a large notch in one end of a shoebox. Cover the notch with foil and poke a single pinhole in the center of the foil. Tape white paper to the opposite end of the box. Standing with the sun behind you, focus the sunlight coming through the pinhole on the opposite side of the shoebox to see an inverted image of the sun.

Rosalind Franklin

DNA STRUCTURE

HIGH SCORER

Born in London, England, in 1920, Rosalind Franklin was the second of five children. A bright child who loved math and solved equations for fun, Rosalind was athletic as well. She played cricket and field hockey in school, although her music instructor, the composer Gustav Holst, wrote to her parents that she was not skilled in that particular area of study.

ROCKS FULL OF HOLES

In college, Rosalind studied chemistry, French, and German. After graduating, she studied the porous properties of coal, which was important in the development of charcoal filters for gas masks used during World War II. She received her PhD from Cambridge for this work.

X-RAY VISION

When the war was over, Dr. Franklin went work in a French lab that studied different compounds using X-ray diffraction, a technique that bounces energetic rays off of objects to make images. She focused her X-rays on coal and then on graphite. Soon she was an expert in a technique called X-ray crystallography, which aims X-rays at crystals to form an image on film, making it possible to determine the structure of molecules.

A TWISTED LADDER

In 1950 Dr. Franklin was working as the X-ray diffraction expert at a lab at Kings College in England, where she was attempting to take a picture of DNA to help scientists understand its structure. DNA is also called the blueprint of life because it is like a map for living things to reproduce themselves. Franklin's background in chemistry came in handy for expertly preparing DNA samples, and she captured what is now called "Photo 51": the first clear image of DNA. The clear "X" shape of the image, paired with her measurements, revealed that DNA has a spiral geometry and hinted at the distance between atoms. Soon after being shown Dr. Franklin's photograph, without her permission, scientists James Watson and Francis Crick were able to put together their famous double-helix model of DNA.

GONE BUT NOT FORGOTTEN

In her lifetime, Rosalind Franklin was given little, if any credit for her essential contribution to solving DNA's structure. Watson's descriptions of Dr. Franklin in his memoir *The Double Helix* were sexist and dismissive. She died young of cancer, and just four years after her death, Watson, Crick, and Wilkins were awarded the Nobel Prize for their work on DNA. Fortunately, today most scientists understand the essential role Franklin played in solving DNA's structure. She also made important contributions to the study of another chemical called RNA and helped decipher the structure of viruses.

IN TODAY'S WORLD

Dr. Franklin's role in the discovery of the structure of deoxyribonucleic acid (DNA) helped lay the foundation for modern molecular biology, which is our understanding of life at the molecular level.

TRY THIS AT HOME!

Use pipe cleaners (chenille sticks) and cotton swabs to create a long, flexible ladder. Look at a picture of DNA structure and twist the ladder you created into a double-helical shape. Observe the double helix from one end to see the shape Rosalind Franklin photographed.

Margaret S. Collins

ZOOLOGY/TERMITES

AN EXPLORER

As a girl, Margaret Collins loved to explore in the woods near her house in West Virginia. Born in 1922, she was the fourth of five children. Her parents both attended college, and her father had gone on to receive a master's degree. Her mother, who had wanted to be an archaeologist, wasn't able to complete her undergraduate degree, but she taught her children the importance of education, a lesson that Margaret never forgot.

CHILD PRODIGY

By the age of six, Margaret's advanced intellect was already evident. She was called a child prodigy, given a library card at the West Virginia State College Library, and allowed to skip two grades. When she was only fourteen years old, Margaret graduated from high school and went to college. Graduating with a degree in biology, she also earned minors in physics and German.

STUCK IN THE LAB

Margaret completed her PhD at the University of Chicago in the lab of Alfred E. Emerson, a termite expert. Not only was Emerson an expert, but he had the largest collection of termites in the world. Emerson was a good mentor and shielded Margaret from some of the racism she faced. Unfortunately, like many male scientists at that time, he didn't want a woman doing field work with him, so while he chased down interesting termites, Margaret was stuck in the laboratory. Despite this, she managed to write an important paper on termites.

A PROFESSOR

Zoology is the branch of biology that studies the animal kingdom. When she got her PhD, Dr. Collins became the first African American woman entomologist and the third female African American zoologist. She went to work as a professor at Howard University but left because men and women weren't treated equally. She later worked for Florida A&M and spent a year at the University of Minnesota before returning to Howard University. During these years, she was fighting hard for civil rights.

GETTING INTO THE FIELD

By this time, Dr. Margaret Collins had come to think of herself as a field biologist and loved traveling the world to study termites in their natural habitat. In 1989, she discovered a new species of termite in Florida, called the Florida damp wood termite. She died in the Cayman Islands in 1996 at the age of seventy-three, doing what she loved best: studying termites.

IN TODAY'S WORLD

Scientists today still study termites, but not just because they can be destructive. Companies are attempting to duplicate termite saliva for industrial use, because it makes termite mounds so strong. Researchers are also interested in the structure of termite mounds, which stay cool inside when it's hot outdoors.

TRY THIS AT HOME!

Mix 1/4 cup (85 g) water, 1/2 cup (170 g) washable glue, and 1/4 cup (85 g) cornstarch together to make a solution resembling termite saliva. On a foil-covered baking sheet, add 2 tablespoons (28 g) termite saliva to 1/2 cup (170 g) dried coffee grounds and shape the mixture into a termite mound. Try adding different amounts of termite saliva to coffee grounds to find the best mix for creating a strong mound. Dry and compare.

Esther Lederberg

LAMBDA PHAGE/REPLICA PLATING

THE GREAT DEPRESSION

Esther Miriam Zimmer was born in the Bronx of New York in 1922. She was seven years old when the Great Depression struck. Esther recalled being hungry as a child and often having just a piece of bread, topped with juice squeezed from a tomato, for lunch. She was very close to her grandfather, who taught her to speak Hebrew.

STRUGGLING SCIENTIST

When she was sixteen, Esther graduated from high school and won a scholarship to study at Hunter College, City University of New York. She loved literature, music, and French, but decided to study biochemistry. After college, she moved to California to pursue a master's degree in genetics at Stanford. To pay rent and buy food, she worked as a laboratory assistant and did laundry for her landlady.

MADISON, WISCONSIN

In 1946, Esther married a scientist named Joshua Lederberg and took his last name. They moved to Madison, Wisconsin, where Joshua had been offered a job as a professor. Despite her master's degree and doctorate research at Stanford, Esther could only find work as Joshua's unpaid laboratory assistant. At the University of Wisconsin, she and Joshua did groundbreaking research on bacteria, and in 1959 they returned to Stanford, where Joshua was made a tenured professor. Even with a PhD and several major discoveries, Esther worked for fifteen years as a senior scientist before she was made an adjunct professor and was named the head of Stanford's Plasmid Reference Center.

A MAJOR DISCOVERY

Around 1950, as she finished her doctorate degree, Esther discovered that the E. coli bacteria she was studying had been infected by a type of virus called a bacteriophage. She named her discovery lambda phage and her research revealed that it was special because it could insert itself into the DNA of the host bacteria. While studying lambda phage, she also found a DNA sequence in bacteria that allows them to exchange DNA with other bacteria.

REPLICA PLATING

Dr. Esther Lederberg created an important laboratory technique called replica plating, which used a velvet stamp pad to transfer bacteria colonies from one plate to another in the exact same pattern. Using this method, scientists can easily find bacteria that have undergone spontaneous DNA mutations, which allow them to grow on plates containing antibiotics.

IN TODAY'S WORLD

Lambda phage is an important tool for molecular biologists and is used in research labs around the world every day.

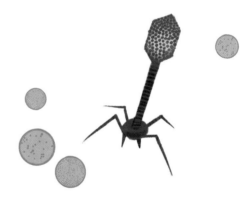

* BIOLOGY *

TRY THIS AT HOME!

Draw identical circles on a piece of paper. Use a stamp to transfer ink from a stamp pad to each of the circles without re-dipping in the ink. This is a model of how bacterial colonies can be transferred from one agar plate to another in the exact same pattern for research.

Edith Flanigen

MOLECULAR SIEVES

A MARVELOUS MENTOR

Edith Flanigen, who was born in 1929 in Buffalo, New York, credits her love of chemistry to a high school teacher. Edith recalls, "She really made (science) exciting. We did hands-on laboratory work, and I think I fell in love with chemistry at that time." Inspired by their teacher, Edith and her two sisters graduated from high school and went on to study chemistry at a nearby college. Following graduation, Edith and her sister, Joan, went on to get master's degrees in chemistry from Syracuse University.

CHEMICAL SPONGES AND EMERALDS

The early 1950s found Flanigen and her sisters working at Union Carbide Corporation, despite the fact that there were very few women working in chemistry at the time. Flanigen focused her research on identifying and purifying silicone polymers, which are compounds made up of repeating patterns of similar chemical units. Eventually she moved into a lab that studied molecular sieves, which are like chemical sponges that can mop up small particles while keeping large ones out. Besides working on molecular sieves, Flanigen co-invented synthetic emeralds that were manufactured by Union Carbide and used in pre-laser technology and in jewelry for a few years. She loved the creative, collaborative environment in industry and helped to foster those ideals in the labs where she worked.

ZEOLITE

In 1973, Flanigen became the first woman named Corporate Research Fellow at Union Carbide, and she eventually reached the highest possible technical positions that could be achieved at the corporations where she worked. During her career, she invented and co-invented more than 200 synthetic materials. Her name appears on more than 100 patents, which protect new inventions from being copied and sold by someone other than the inventor. Flannigan's research on molecular sieves was especially important. Filtering molecules (groups of atoms) by size allows scientists and industries to separate chemicals compounds. Edith's work with sieve materials called zeolites made it possible to refine oil into its usable parts more safely and efficiently.

PRESIDENTIAL RECOGNITION

In 1983, Flanigen received a PhD from D'Youville College. Besides being inducted into the National Inventors Hall of Fame in 2004, Dr. Edith Flanigan has received countless awards for her work. In 1992 she became the first woman ever awarded the Perkin Medal, and in 2014 President Barack Obama presented her with the National Medal of Technology and Innovation.

IN TODAY'S WORLD

Dr. Flanigen is the foremost authority on zeolite chemistry, and her work is the basis of the molecular sieve industry, which produces chemicals we use every day, including laundry detergent and cat litter.

TRY THIS AT HOME!

Outside, pour a mixture of sand and gravel into a kitchen sieve. Use a hose to rinse the mixture. Notice how sand and small stone pass through the sieve, while larger ones are trapped. This is a model of how molecular sieves can be used to trap and separate certain chemical compounds.

CHEMISTRY

Tu Youyou

MEDICINAL PLANT COMPOUNDS

AN INTERRUPTED EDUCATION

Tu Youyou was born in a city on the east coast of China into a family that put a high value on education. The only girl in her family, she attended the best schools in the region until she became sick with tuberculosis when she was sixteen. By the time she had recovered and returned to school two years later, Tu had decided to study medicine so that she could stay healthy and help others. After graduating from high school, she was accepted into the school of pharmacy at the Medical School of Peking University.

PLANTS AS MEDICINE

In her pharmacy courses, Tu learned to study traditional Chinese remedies through the lens of Western medicine. Her professors taught her to identify and classify plants based on their botanical descriptions along with methods for extracting chemical compounds from them. Tu also learned how to characterize the structures of the chemicals she'd isolated. This education helped her to understand how some traditional plants are able to cure disease. Her first research project involved studying the effect of an herb called *Lobelia chinensus* on a disease caused by a parasitic flatworm.

A BROKEN FAMILY

Dr. Youyou left her two young daughters in the care of relatives so she could travel to a laboratory to search for a cure for malaria. Malaria is a deadly disease caused by a parasite spread by mosquitos, and the parasite had become resistant to a number of available medicines. Youyou searched through ancient Chinese texts and folk recipes, searching for new compounds to test against the malaria parasite. She collected more than 2,000 prescriptions to test and went to work experimenting with them.

A CURE

After a number of failures, an herb in the *Artemisia* family showed promising results, but she couldn't repeat them consistently. Going back through old books, she found a recipe that contained a cure for malaria fever that called for "A handful of Qinghao immersed in two liters of water, wring out the juice and drink it all." Dr. Youyou realized that most of the recipes had called for boiling the plant, which may have destroyed the chemical capable of killing the malaria parasite. She followed the heat-free recipe and it killed malaria parasites, so she isolated the fraction containing the active chemical. Due to limited resources, she and two of her colleagues tested the toxicity of the compound by drinking it themselves and found it to be safe enough for clinical trials.

A PRIZE

In 2015 Tu Youyou won the Nobel Prize in Physiology or Medicine for her discovery of artemisinin, a new therapy for malaria.

IN TODAY'S WORLD

Dr. Tu Youyou's discovery has saved millions of lives and is still used today to treat malaria all around the world.

TRY THIS AT HOME!

Peel off the bottom of an aloe vera leaf. Use a spoon to remove the gel inside. Refrigerate the aloe vera gel in a jar and use it to sooth irritated skin and sunburn.

June Almeida

CORONAVIRUSES/AGGLUTINATION

A NEW VIRUS

When June Almeida wrote a paper about a new virus she'd discovered, scientists reviewing her paper told her that she'd made a mistake. June, who was one of the world's most skilled electron microscope technicians, would soon prove them wrong. She had, in fact, photographed and identified an entirely new kind of virus, which she and her colleagues later named coronavirus.

STRAIGHT TO WORK

Born in Scotland in 1930, June was a bright student, but she didn't have enough money to go to the university. When she was sixteen, she left school and went to work as a laboratory technician at a hospital, where she looked through a microscope for the first time. June proved extremely talented at histopathology, which involves studying slides of human tissue and identifying diseases.

ELECTRON MICROSCOPY

She eventually went to work in a lab in London, got married, and moved to Canada where she learned to use electron microscopes, which are powerful enough to magnify viruses. Although she didn't have a college degree, June quickly became so talented at microscopy that researchers she worked with made her a co-author on some important scientific papers about the structures of viruses.

CLUMPING VIRUSES

A British professor of virology named A. P. Waterson convinced June to return to England, where she was awarded a Doctor of Science degree. Now called Dr. Almeida, June became the first person to visualize the rubella virus, which causes the German measles. She also pioneered a technique called *immune electron microscopy*, which uses antibodies to clump viral particles together so that they're easier to see.

A HALO

When a colleague sent her a sample of an unidentified virus to look at with her electron microscope, June thought it looked similar to the one she'd tried to publish a paper about before. This time people believed her when she said that she'd discovered an entirely new kind of virus. She and her colleagues named this new family of viruses coronaviruses, for the crown-like halo that was visible around the viral particles in June's photographs.

Later in her career, Dr. Almeida published important papers on a bird respiratory virus and the hepatitis B virus. She also came out of retirement in the 1980s to help take images of HIV, which causes the disease AIDS.

IN TODAY'S WORLD

Thanks to the work of June Almeida and her colleagues, scientists were recently able to identify the SARS virus and the SARS-CoV2 virus that causes COVID-19 as coronaviruses. What Dr. Almeida and her colleagues discovered about the structure of these and other viruses still helps scientists develop vaccines and drugs to keep humans and animals safe from them today.

TRY THIS AT HOME!

Make models of coronaviruses by rolling Play-Doh into several small balls. Use another color to cover each ball with tiny Play-Doh spikes. These spikes form a crown-like halo in photographs and are the reason for the virus's name, since "corona" is borrowed from the Latin word for crown.

Sylvia Earle

OCEAN RESEARCH

POND EXPLORER

The ocean first got American oceanographer Sylvia Earle's attention when she was three years old, and a wave knocked her off her feet. She's been running back into the water ever since. Born in 1935, Sylvia lived on a farm in New Jersey with her parents and two brothers until she was thirteen. A nature lover, she spent her free time exploring the life in their back-yard pond, catching fish and tadpoles to keep in jars where she could observe them more closely. When her family moved to Florida, her interest immediately shifted to the wildlife in the Gulf of Mexico.

SCUBA

Sylvia was such a dedicated student that she graduated from high school when she was sixteen and got a scholarship to Florida State University. Interested in marine plants, she became a certified SCUBA diver to study her subjects close-up. Sylvia went to graduate school at Duke University and focused her research on plants called algae, which live in the water and turn carbon dioxide and sunlight into oxygen and sugars. After pausing her education to have two children, she completed her PhD in botany (the study of plants), collecting more than 20,000 samples of algae from the Gulf of Mexico. She was one of the first biologists to use SCUBA to document ocean organisms.

LIFE UNDER WATER

It was unusual for women to join ocean research expeditions at that time, but Sylvia joined several, accompanying research crews on voyages to the Galápagos Islands, the Chilean coast, and the Panama Canal Zone. She did all this while raising two children, taking classes, and writing her PhD dissertation. Sylvia continued to dive on expeditions around the world and was the first woman to set foot in an underwater habitat where scientists lived 100 feet (30.5 m) below the surface. In 1970, she led an all-female team to live and dive 50 feet (15 m) under water in the Tektite II Project, near the U.S. Virgin Islands.

A DEEP DIVE

Sylvia dove with sperm whales for the 1980 film *Gentle Giants of the Pacific*. In 1979, she famously rode a submarine to the ocean floor off the coast of Hawaii. Wearing a pressurized "JIM" suit, she was carried down 1,250 feet (381 m), deeper than anyone has ever walked the ocean floor untethered. Detaching from the submarine, she walked along the bottom for two and a half hours. Far from the sun's light, the water was inky black and she was surrounded by glowing bioluminescent creatures. Sylvia said that the experience was like diving into a galaxy of lights.

NOAA

Sylvia was the first woman to be chief scientist of the U.S. National Ocean and Atmospheric Administration (NOAA). In 1998, she was named *Time* magazine's first Hero for the Planet. Passionate about protecting the ocean, Sylvia wants people to understand how important it is to all of us. She says, "You should treat the ocean as if your life depended on it, because it does!" and reminds people that "with every breath they take, with every drop of water they drink, the ocean is touching them."

IN TODAY'S WORLD

Dr. Sylvia Earle continues to educate the public about our oceans and leads Mission Blue, which is working to inspire "an upwelling of public awareness, access and support for a worldwide network of marine protected areas."

* ECOLOGY *

TRY THIS AT HOME!

Fill a bowl with water and add a few drops of blue food coloring. Put one to two table-spoons (14–28 g) of vegetable oil on the surface of the water to represent an oil spill. Float a feather on the surface of the oil to see what happens to birds when oil spills occur. Experiment with different techniques for removing oil from the water.

Ada Yonath

RIBOSOME STRUCTURE

FALLING FOR SCIENCE

Ada Yonath set the stage for her scientific career early on. During an ill-conceived childhood experiment, she broke her arm falling from a stack of furniture she was using to measure the height of a balcony. Ada also recalls being inspired at a young age by a biography of Marie Curie.

A STRUGGLE

Ada Yonath's parents were from Poland, but they had left their home country to move to Jerusalem, where they struggled with poverty. Her father suffered from life-threatening health problems, but he and her mother had big dreams for Ada and did everything possible to ensure that she got a good education. After he died when she was only eleven, Ada and her mother worked for a year trying to make ends meet before moving to Tel Aviv around 1951 to be closer to relatives who could help them.

INTRODUCTION TO CRYSTALLOGRAPHY

In college Ada studied chemistry, biochemistry, and biophysics before going on to work toward her PhD at the Weismann Institute of Science. For her doctorate research, she studied the structure of a protein called collagen using X-ray crystallography, which bombards crystals with X-rays to determine their structure. After being awarded her PhD, she did postdoctoral research in the United States before returning home to establish the first biological crystallography laboratory in Israel.

MOUNT EVEREST

In the late 1970s, Dr. Yonath decided to tackle a monumental project. She wanted to discover the three-dimensional structure of ribosomes, which are the cellular machines that translate genetic material called RNA into proteins. Ribosomes are complex structures made up of two parts called subunits, and although many scientists told her that what she'd proposed couldn't be done, Ada was determined. Later, she compared her research journey to "climbing Mt. Everest only to discover that a higher Everest stood in front of us."

POLAR BEARS AND RIBOSOMES

To study the structure of ribosomes, first Dr. Yonath had to discover how to crystallize them. After reading about how the ribosomes in polar bears become neatly stacked during hibernation, Dr. Yonath got the idea to isolate organized ribosomes from bacteria that live in extremely cold, hot, or radioactive environments. She figured out how to flash freeze these crystallized ribosome structures and bombard them with X-rays. In 2001 Ada Yonath was awarded the Nobel Prize for discovering the structure and function of the ribosome.

IN TODAY'S WORLD

Today, Dr. Yonath's work has proved essential for the production of new antibiotics.

TRY THIS AT HOME!

Ribosomes are blob-like structures that read code from a molecule called RNA to make amino acids, which are the building blocks of proteins. Thread ring-shaped candy or cereal on a piece of yarn to see how ribosomes assemble chains of amino acids. Once they exit ribosomes, amino acid chains are folded into three-dimensional proteins.

Wangari Maathai
GREEN BELT MOVEMENT

KIKUYU KNOWLEDGE
Wangari Maathai was born in 1940 and grew up in the Kikuyu community in the central highlands of Kenya, surrounded by natural beauty in the countryside. She recalled her mother telling her not to collect firewood from fig trees, which were sacred to their people. When she got older, Wangari realized that those special trees protected the sloping landscape.

A DOCTORATE DEGREE
After attending primary school in Kenya, Wangari went to Mount St. Scholastic College in Kansas, where she majored in biology. Next, she earned a master's degree in biology from the University of Pittsburgh, in Pennsylvania. Returning to Africa, she attended the University of Nairobi and became the first woman in East Africa to earn a doctorate degree.

A CHANGED LANDSCAPE
While in the United States, Wangari was greatly influenced by the civil rights movement, and in graduate school she became a member of the National Council of Women. At one of their meetings, she learned what was happening to the environment in her beloved Kenya, which had changed dramatically over the five years when she was in America. After gaining independence from British rule, Kenya's newly independent government embraced commercial agriculture, cutting down trees to plant cash crops and build new housing developments.

DESERTIFICATION
Trees had been cut down, streams had been drying up, the water was polluted, and harvests had not been good. Women had to walk long distances to find firewood for cooking and boiling water and worried about feeding their families. Wangari understood that trees hold soil and water in place after it rains. She recognized that many of the problems in her country were the direct result of deforestation. Agriculture and development were turning fertile land into desert.

THE GREEN BELT MOVEMENT
To help solve the environmental problems, Wangari helped found the Green Belt Movement, which promised to plant millions of trees throughout Kenya. She understood that planting trees would help restore ecosystems and provide food and fuel for communities. She also fought against cutting down more forest for building and housing developments. Much of the deforestation had been done illegally, with the blessing of a corrupt government. Wangari was threatened, beaten, and even sent to jail, but she never gave up and mobilized thousands of women and men to plant trees.

52 MILLION NEW TREES
Through the simple act of planting trees, Wangari Maathai understood that ecology is more than a scientific discipline. It is a matter of war, peace, human rights, and the survival of species, including ours. In 2004, she was awarded the Nobel Peace Prize. The Green Belt Movement has already planted more than 52 million trees. Wangari died in 2011.

IN TODAY'S WORLD
Trees are very efficient at removing carbon dioxide from the atmosphere. With climate change, it is now more important than ever that we stop deforestation and plant trees to replace those that have been cut down.

TRY THIS AT HOME!
Look up information about tree seeds found in your area that are easy to grow, such as maple seeds. Find a tree seed and plant it in a flowerpot. Keep the soil damp so it can germinate and grow. When it is large enough, plant the seedling outdoors in a spot where there is plenty of room for it to grow.

Patricia Bath

MEDICAL DEVICES/CATARACT SURGERY

A CHEMISTRY SET

Patricia Bath was born in the Harlem neighborhood of New York City in 1942. Her father was a subway train operator and her mother worked as a housekeeper when she wasn't taking care of Patricia and her brother, so she could save money for her children's education. Patricia's parents always encouraged her to work hard in school, and her mother sparked her interest in science when she bought Patricia her first chemistry set.

A SCIENCE-LOVER

Patricia was an outstanding math and science student in high school, and she discovered that she loved biology. When she was sixteen, cancer cell research she did at a workshop sponsored by the National Science Foundation was so impressive that it was included in an academic paper. After earning a BA in chemistry, she attended Howard University's College of Medicine, where she received her medical degree in 1967. Following the assassination of Martin Luther King Jr. that same year, she organized her fellow medical students to volunteer their time and talents to help people in their community who could not afford health care.

AN OPHTHALMOLOGIST

When Patricia, now Dr. Bath, returned home to work at Harlem Hospital, she noticed there were more blind patients there than they were at a neighboring hospital where she also worked. She continued her education, doing a residency to become an ophthalmologist, which is an expert in eyes and vision. When Dr. Bath's research demonstrated that certain groups of people suffered from more eye problems than others, she wanted to understand why and help address the problem. She set up an eye clinic at Harlem Hospital Center, where they started doing eye surgeries. In 1972, Patricia got married and had a daughter named Eraka.

AN INVENTOR

After moving to Los Angeles, Dr. Bath continued working to improve surgical treatment for blind patients. She invented a medical device that dissolves cloudy lenses called cataracts, which can form on the eyes of older people. Once the cataracts are gone, new lenses can be put in. She patented four more devices for eye surgeries, and thanks to her inventions, people who were blind for decades were able to regain their eyesight. Throughout her career, Dr. Bath addressed issues in society that contributed to vision problems, such as poverty and inadequate access to health care. Dr. Patricia Bath was a partner of the American Institute of Blindness, whose motto is "Eyesight is a basic human right." She died in 2019.

IN TODAY'S WORLD

Dr. Bath's contributions to surgical equipment and eye care are still used in eye clinics around the world every day.

TRY THIS AT HOME!

Use waxed paper held in place by rubber bands to cover the ends of two toilet paper tubes and look through them. This will help you to understand how cloudy lenses, called cataracts, make it hard for some people to see. Replace the waxed paper with saran wrap and look through the tubes again. Now, you will be able to observe how cataract surgery improves vision by replacing the cloudy lenses with clear new ones.

Christine Darden

AIRCRAFT WING DESIGN

A TEACHER'S KID

Christine Mann was born in 1920 in Monroe, North Carolina. Her father sold insurance. Christine's mother, a teacher, began bringing Christine to school when she was three years old. By the time she was four, Christine had started kindergarten. Soon, she discovered a passion for taking things apart and putting them back together. Breaking down and rebuilding her bike was one of her first projects.

CIVIL RIGHTS

After graduating as the valedictorian of her high school class, Christine attended Hampton University in Virginia. While she was there, she became involved in the early civil rights movement and attended some sit-ins with her classmates. She graduated in 1962 with a degree in mathematics and taught high school for a few years.

AEROSOL PHYSICS

When she was a teacher, Christine married Walter Darden and changed her last name. She got a job in an aerosol physics lab, studying the aerodynamics of how tiny particles move through the air. While working in the lab, she also taught and earned a master's degree in mathematics from Virginia State University.

A HUMAN COMPUTER

In 1967, Christine was hired by NASA to work as one of their "human computers," a group of women who solved mathematical equations for engineers working in the Space Race to safely send humans into space and bring them back to Earth. The Black women working as computers were segregated from the white women with the same jobs. To make doing the calculations more efficient, Christine wrote programs for the early computers at Langley Research Center, where she worked. She and the women she worked with played an integral role in making NASA's first space missions possible.

A GOOD QUESTION

When Christine asked the director at NASA why men were made engineers, while equally qualified women were not given the same opportunity, he was surprised. Nobody had ever asked him the question before. Christine Darden was transferred to the engineering team, earned a PhD in engineering from George Washington University, and was the first African American appointed to the highest rank at Langley Research Center.

SONIC BOOM

In her role as the leader of Langley's Sonic Boom Team, she used computer programs to test aircraft designs. One of Dr. Darden's main jobs was to redesign super-fast aircraft to reduce the shock waves they can cause in the atmosphere. The name *sonic boom* refers to the thunderous sound made by air molecules crashing together when an object moves faster than the speed of sound. She also tested models of airplanes in wind tunnels to study their aerodynamics.

HIDDEN FIGURE

Christine Darden retired in 2007, but she continues to serve as a role model for young mathematicians, scientists, and engineers. She advises aspiring engineers to picture themselves in their dream job, plan, prepare, and persist. Her story was featured in the film *Hidden Figures*.

IN TODAY'S WORLD

NASA is still working to design supersonic aircraft that produce less noise and environmental impact.

TRY THIS AT HOME!

Look up instructions for how to fold a paper airplane and test how far it will fly. Then, change the wing and tail design to see whether you can engineer a plane that will fly farther. Try the same thing with other paper airplane designs.

Margaret Cairns Etter

CRYSTALLOGRAPHY

SCIENCE WITH A SMILE

Born in 1943 and nicknamed "Peggy," Margaret Carins Etter loved people and science. She especially liked people who do science. Her students, friends, and co-workers recall her laugh echoing down hallways and the smiley-face stickers she jokingly gave colleagues when they got good results in the lab. Etter was famous for always doing what she considered to be the right thing, even if it meant risking her career, and she made enormous contributions to science in a relatively short amount of time.

10,000 LAKES

Peggy Etter was born in Delaware, and her father was a chemist at DuPont Experimental Station. She grew up surrounded by scientists who worked with her dad, and she went to the University of Pennsylvania to study chemistry. After earning a master's degree at the University of Delaware, Peggy moved to Minnesota, the Land of 10,000 Lakes, where she earned a PhD and settled down to teach for a year at Augustana College before going to work at 3M.

THE BIG PICTURE

Eventually, Dr. Etter returned to the University of Minnesota where she became a full professor and dove into more research. She made important discoveries by studying hydrogen bonding patterns in chemical structures, rather than focusing on individual bonds. Etter was also fascinated by crystal growth and was one of the first scientists to observe and investigate the strange phenomenon of "jumping crystals," which are now studied in a field of chemistry called mechanochemistry.

AN ADVOCATE

As she explored the mysteries of the unknown on her laboratory bench, Etter fought against oppressive traditions in the worlds of industry and academia. According to her colleagues, Etter believed that actions spoke louder than words and wasn't afraid to push the boundaries. She spoke at schools to encourage girls to get into science, helped to establish the 3M Visiting Women's Scientist program, and was a director and instructor in their STEP program, which encourages minority students to become scientists.

A LASTING IMPRESSION

Although Dr. Etter died when she was only forty-nine, she left the chemistry world a better place. Her former students, colleagues, and close friends wrote a number of tributes to her, recalling her "intelligence, elegant presentation, enthusiasm, and radiant personality" and the fact that "she demonstrated what it meant to show respect and compassion for everyone, irrespective of status or behavior."

IN TODAY'S WORLD

Each year, the University of Minnesota holds an annual Etter Memorial Lecture and the American Crystallographic Association gives two awards in honor of Dr. Etter.

TRY THIS AT HOME!

With parental supervision, dissolve three cups (720 g) of Epsom salts in two cups (480 g) of water in the microwave. Cool slightly and pour into three jars. Make three small shapes from pipe cleaners (chenille sticks) and hang each one from a pencil positioned across the jars' mouths so they are suspended in the Epsom solution. Watch the crystals grow and remove the pipe cleaners when they're covered with needle-like salt crystals.

Valerie L. Thomas

ILLUSION TRANSMITTER

A SELF-STARTER
Valerie L. Thomas was born in Maryland in 1943. She first became interested in science while watching her father fix their television set. Valerie checked a book called *The Boys' First Book of Electronics* out of the library. Although her father refused to help her with the projects in the book, Valerie learned what she could on her own.

PHYSICS CLASS
Valerie's family and most of her teachers were not supportive of her interest in science and engineering, but she took a physics class in school. That class, along with the encouragement of a few teachers, kept her interested in the sciences, and she went to college to study physics at Morgan State University, where she was one of only two women majoring in physics.

NASA
After graduating with a physics degree, Valerie went to work at NASA, analyzing data from satellites. She developed computer data systems and oversaw the development of LANDSAT, the longest-running program for collecting satellite data from Earth. Data from these satellites allowed Valerie and her coworkers at NASA to create a system for making predictions about world-wide food crop yields.

ILLUSION TRANSMITTER
An exhibit at a scientific seminar in 1976 caught her attention. Using mirrors, the device gave the illusion that a lightbulb was still glowing, even after it had been turned off. Fascinated, Valerie experimented on her own, using mirrors to produce three-dimensional (3-D) images in front of the glass. In 1977, she used what she'd learned to invent a device called the illusion transmitter. The device, which she patented, was the forerunner of the 3-D technology we use today.

PROBING SPACE
While at NASA, Valerie Thomas became the associate chief of the Space Science Data Operators office. She helped develop technology for NASA's scientific network and the modern internet. Valerie was also involved in projects related to the Voyager Spacecraft, a space probe studying the outer solar system and Halley's Comet.

A ROLE MODEL
Valerie was awarded the Goddard Space Flight Center Award of Merit and NASA's Equal Opportunity Medal. During her career at NASA, and following her retirement in 1995, she made hundreds of school visits, encouraging minorities and women to pursue science and engineering careers.

IN TODAY'S WORLD
Valerie Thomas's ideas are still being used to create modern 3-D technology. The LANDSAT satellite program she created monitors Earth's atmosphere and oceans, tracking climate change. Data coming from these satellites aid the government in everything from land management to helping endangered species.

* PHYSICS *

TRY THIS AT HOME!
Look at your reflection on the back of a spoon. Flip the spoon around so that the image is flipped upside-down (inverted). Your image is inverted because of the way light is reflected by curved, concaved surfaces. This physics can be used to create useful optical illusions.

Jocelyn Bell Burnell

PULSARS

SPUTNIK

Jocelyn Bell Burnell was born in Lurgan, Northern Ireland, in 1923. Her father sparked her interest in the stars by checking out astronomy books from the library and waking Jocelyn and her sister to watch the satellite Sputnik pass overhead. When Jocelyn was thirteen, she went to boarding school in England, where her physics teacher Mr. Tillott encouraged her interest in science.

A BOY'S CLUB

As the only woman studying physics at the University of Glasgow, Jocelyn was harassed by the male students. They whistled, stomped their feet, and banged their desks each time she entered the lecture hall. Jocelyn graduated with honors and a degree in physics, but the experience of feeling so alone stayed with her. From there, she went on to Cambridge University.

A WINDOW TO THE UNIVERSE

Radio physics was a new and exciting field. Bursts of electromagnetic energy from the far reaches of the universe could be detected and recorded as radio signals that made bumps and squiggles on the paper of recording instruments. The farther away objects were, the older they were, so studying far-off objects was like traveling back in time.

SIGNALS FROM SPACE

Jocelyn helped her graduate advisor Anthony Hewish construct a radio telescope that covered four acres and looked like an agricultural frame made of bean poles. While strong signals from deep space registered as strong peaks in the data flowing from the telescope, there were also background radio signals from human activity. Jocelyn was put in charge of running the telescope.

A SQUIGGLE

Every night, Jocelyn went to the university's observatory to analyze signals coming from the radio telescope. She studied 900 feet of paper each day, searching for peaks representing electromagnetic bursts coming from space. One night in 1967, she noticed a funny squiggle on the paper. Similar peaks appeared on the paper several times at regular intervals, indicating rhythmic pulses of energy from deep space.

Jocelyn contacted Dr. Hewish about her discovery, but he did not believe her until he observed the signal himself and they found it on a second telescope. Soon afterwards, she stumbled uninvited into a meeting in which Dr. Hewish and other men were discussing (without her) the origin of the signal she had discovered.

PULSARS

Later that night, Jocelyn marched back out to the observatory in the freezing cold to point the radio telescope at a different part of the night sky, where she recalled seeing a similar signal. She found it immediately, and the second pulsing signal confirmed that the radio waves were not background noise, but came from an entirely new type of star, which they later called a pulsar.

Dr. Jocelyn Bell Burnell's discovery of pulsars changed our understanding of the universe. She was left out, however, when Hewish and Martin Ryle were awarded the 1974 Nobel Prize for Physics. In 2018, she was awarded the Breakthrough Prize and three million dollars, which she donated to the Institute of Physics to increase diversity in the field.

IN TODAY'S WORLD

Pulsars are important tools for physicists, and they are used to test theories of relativity on a cosmic scale.

TRY THIS AT HOME!

Make a model of a pulsar by taping two flashlights pointing in opposite directions onto a ball. Turn the flashlights on and go into a dark room. Spin the ball so the flashlights make a constant, repeating pattern on the wall, representing the radio signals Jocelyn found on her telescope.

Linda Buck

OLFACTORY CHEMISTRY

A HAPPY CHILDHOOD

Linda Buck was born in Seattle, in 1947, to parents who encouraged her creativity from the beginning. With a father who was an electrical engineer and a mother who loved puzzles, Buck was primed for a lifetime of innovative problem-solving. Given the freedom to pursue a number of interests, Linda wasn't sure what she wanted to study in college, but she was drawn to psychology, which is the study of the human mind.

A NONTRADITIONAL PATH

After attending the University of Washington, Linda wasn't sure that she wanted to be a psychotherapist, so she left school to travel but continued taking classes when she could. A course in immunology, which is the science of how our bodies fight infection, got her interested in biology, and she graduated from college with a degree in microbiology and psychology when she was twenty-eight. She moved to Texas to earn a PhD in immunology before going to work in the lab of Richard Axel at Columbia University.

YEARS IN A LAB

In Axel's neuroscience lab, Dr. Buck was fascinated by cells that send signals to the brain, and became obsessed with the idea of figuring out which cells in the nose detect scent. She also wanted to understand which genes (DNA codes) are related to these cells, and how the cells can recognize so many different odors. She worked for years to unravel the mystery, trying everything she could think of, with nothing to show for it.

MYSTERY SOLVED

Dr. Buck could hardly believe it when, in 1991, she discovered a group of genes that no one had ever seen before. These genes coded for a group of 350 smell receptors that work in combination to detect thousands of different odors. In 2004 Linda and her colleague Richard Axel shared the Nobel Prize in Physiology or Medicine for their discoveries of odorant receptors and the organization of the olfactory smell system. She said, "As a woman in science, I sincerely hope that my receiving a Nobel Prize will send a message to young women everywhere that the doors are open to them and that they should follow their dreams."

IN TODAY'S WORLD

Currently, many researchers are working to create "artificial noses" for environmental monitoring, medical diagnosis, and a host of other applications.

TRY THIS AT HOME!

Collect food items, herbs, and/or flowers with strong smells. Put the items on plates. Blindfold a friend or family member to see whether they can identify each object by smell.

Robin Wall Kimmerer

PLANT ECOLOGY/TRADITIONAL KNOWLEDGE

ECOLOGY

THE HEART BERRY

Born in 1953, Robin Wall Kimmerer grew up in Upstate New York. In English, her Potawatomi name means "Light Shining through Sky Woman." The Potawatomi Nation originally lived in the Great Lakes region of the United States, but in the late 1700s, many Potawatomi were forcibly removed by the government to a reservation in Oklahoma. It was nature that helped Robin and her parents reconnect with their Potawatomi heritage. As a girl, she loved exploring the fields and woods and wrote that "it was the wild strawberries, beneath dewy leaves on an almost-summer morning, who gave me my sense of the world, my place in it." According to Robin, "In Potawatomi, the strawberry is 'ode min,' the heart berry. We recognize them as the leaders of the berries, the first to bear fruit."

MOSS

Robin earned a master's degree in botany and then a PhD in plant ecology from the University of Wisconsin, Madison. While studying forest ecology in graduate school, she became fascinated by mosses, which are small plants with no roots. Studying them close-up, she discovered an entire miniature world. After teaching in Kentucky, Robin moved back to Upstate New York to become a professor at State University of New York College of Environmental Science and Forestry (ESF), where she had received her bachelor's degree.

WAYS OF KNOWING

Today, Robin is interested in educating her students and the public about science and traditional ecological knowledge. She wrote an award-winning book called *Gathering Moss: A Natural and Culture History of Mosses*, which beautifully weaves plant ecology into Robin's understanding of traditional knowledge, or "ways of knowing." Robin is also the director of the Center for Native Peoples and the Environment at ESF. The program gives Indigenous students more opportunities to study environmental science and allows traditional science to benefit from the wisdom of Native philosophy. Robin hopes that the center will help us reach the common goal of sustainability.

WORDS MATTER

Dr. Robin Wall Kimmerer thinks that language is extremely important. As a writer and a scientist, she is interested in "not only the restoration of ecological communities, but restoration of our relationships to land." She believes that our words affect our behavior and our attitude about the world. Rather than referring to the Earth as a thing, or "it," she suggests that we refer to our planet and everything natural thing on it as family, or "kin." She hopes that once we stop seeing nature as separate from ourselves, we will take better care of our world.

A MOTHER, A SCIENTIST, A WRITER, AND A MEMBER OF A FIRST NATION

Robin writes, "Knowing that you love the Earth changes you, activates you to protect and defend and celebrate. But when you feel that the Earth loves you in return, that feeling transforms the relationship from a one-way street into a sacred bond." Her identity as a mother, a scientist, a writer, and a member of a First Nation has made her a social activist for the environment, sustainability, social justice, and Native American issues.

IN TODAY'S WORLD

Dr. Robin Wall Kimmerer's award-winning book, *Braiding Sweetgrass*, beautifully illustrates the interdependence of humans and the natural world.

TRY THIS AT HOME!

Take a magnifying glass along and go on a hunt for velvety green and brown mosses. Mosses can be found almost everywhere: in yards, in woods, on old shingles, and even on rocks. Observe the mosses you find under the magnifying glass to get a closer look at their structure.

Dana Bergstrom

ANTARCTIC RESEARCH

NATURE LOVER

In Sydney, Australia, Dana Bergstrom knew she wanted to be scientist when she was five years old. After school, she'd climb trees and create miniature African landscapes populated with plastic lions and elephants. Sometimes, Dana's mom took her and her sister to Manly Beach to explore tide pools. Dana also loved pouring over the photographs in *National Geographic* and an atlas of the world, which contained drawings of plants, minerals, and dinosaurs.

A WOMAN IN THE FIELD

By the time she was twelve, Dana knew that she wanted to be an ecologist. After high school, she pursued her dream by completing undergraduate and graduate degrees at Macquarie University. At that time, there were mostly men in the Australian Antarctic program, but she forged a new path as one of the first female scientists to travel south to do fieldwork over a long period of time.

AN ENDANGERED ECOSYSTEM

To do research for her master's degree and PhD, Dana traveled to Macquarie Island in the southwestern Pacific Ocean. About halfway between New Zealand and Antarctica, it is one of the cloudiest places on Earth. Part of the Antipodes Subantarctic Islands tundra ecoregion, Macquarie Island is home to the world's entire royal penguin population during their annual nesting season and has an interesting ecological history. Dana was focused on studying unique vegetation on the island, but while she was there, other native species were struggling for survival due to invasive rats, cats, and rabbits brought to the island by European ships.

NEVER WAKE A SLEEPING FUR SEAL

One day, while doing research on a remote, volcanic subarctic island named Heard Island, Dana had a close encounter with a grumpy male fur seal, whom she accidentally woke from a nap. Dana stood her ground and shouted as the enormous animal charged, but the seal wasn't deterred and kept coming toward her, snorting and foaming at the mouth. Deciding to run, Dana slipped in an elephant seal wallow and fell into a smelly, slimy depression in the ground. Luckily, this brought her to a lower level than the fur seal. After looking at Dana with a satisfied face, the fur seal rocked back and forth from flipper to flipper as if he were laughing and then returned to his sleeping spot and resumed his nap.

THE 3AS

Dr. Dana Bergstrom works tirelessly to educate the public about the importance of caring for Antarctica. She has identified what she calls the 3As: awareness, anticipation, and action, which are all crucial to conserving the natural world. Dana also used her artistic skills to write a musical called *Antarctica, Beneath the Storm*, which is about a female penguin biologist who travels to Antarctica and experiences the realities of climate change. In 2021, she won the 2021 Eureka Prize for Leadership in Innovation and Science.

IN TODAY'S WORLD

Today, as a senior researcher at the Australian Antarctic Division, Dana is interested in identifying any risks against Antarctic and sub-Antarctic ecosystems and finding ways to keep ecosystems from collapsing in the future. She helped design a biosecurity center at a wharf that serves as Australia's gateway to Antarctica to help keep invasive plant and animal species out.

TRY THIS AT HOME!

Sprinkle some grass seeds on a concrete sidewalk or driveway. Get the bottom of your shoes muddy and walk over the grass seeds to see how many seeds stick to your shoes. This exercise demonstrates how easily humans can spread plants from one place to another.

Aparajita Datta

SEED DISPERSAL

* ECOLOGY *

A PASSION FOR BOOKS AND ANIMALS

Aparajita Datta was born in Kolkata, the capital of the Indian state of West Bengal, in 1970. When she was eight, her family moved to Lusaka, Zambia, in southern Africa. Her interest in animals was first inspired by the books of James Herriot and Gerald Durrell and one of her teachers invited her to join the Zoo Club at school. After five years, Aparajita's family returned to India, where she finished high school and studied botany at Presidency University.

THE PAKKE TIGER RESERVE

After graduating from college, Aparajita earned a master's degree from the Wildlife Institute of India. While she was in graduate school, she met Charudutt Mishra, who was also studying wildlife ecology, and they married. In 1995, she went to the Pakke Tiger Reserve in Northeast India to study how logging was affecting wildlife. While she was there, Aparajita became fascinated by hornbill birds and continued to study them for her PhD.

HORNBILLS

Hornbills are beautiful birds with long bills that sometimes look like the horn of a cow. Their beaks are often very colorful and sometimes have a bony protrusion on top. Aparajita's research revealed that hornbills are more than just pretty birds. The birds she studied in the Pakhui Wildlife Sanctuary turned out to be vital participants in the ecosystems they inhabited, spreading the seeds of more than eighty species of trees. In fact, some tree seeds were only spread by hornbills. Aparajita calls hornbills the "farmers of the forest."

SEED DISPERSAL

"Understanding connections and interactions between animals and plants is the part of my work I find most exciting," Aparajita says. "In tropical forests, 80 to 90 percent of tree species bear fruits that animals disperse. But . . . many large mammals and birds like the hornbill—crucial to seed dispersal—are hunted. Some parts of the park have become empty forests, devoid of wildlife. The absence of these dispersers could have severe consequences for the regeneration of many plant species."

PROTECTING HORNBILLS

Aparajita continued to study wildlife in the Arunachal region, which includes the Pakke Tiger Reserve. She did a wildlife census in the area, counting tigers, bears, clouded leopards, and deer in the park. She studied hornbills as well, because they were in grave danger of extinction due to hunting and the cutting down of trees where they nested. Aparajita started to work with the Lisu and Nyishi people in the area, enlisting former hunters to help protect the birds and their nests.

LEARNING FROM THE LISU PEOPLE

Passionate about nurturing people's relationship with the wild, Aparajita set up a nest adoption program. She formed a partnership between people in the cities who offered financial support and people who live in the forest, who protected hornbills. She said, "The Lisu people are right by our side. They've shown and told me things I never would have otherwise known. I think wildlife biologists often forget how much we depend on the insight of local people. To me, part of the wonder of this incredible place is being there with the Lisu, sharing moments in the forest with them." In 2016, the Pakke Tiger Reserve won an India Biodiversity Award for its Hornbill Nest Adoption Program.

IN TODAY'S WORLD

In addition to studying and helping to protect hornbills, Dr. Aparajita Datta is working on projects to restore native tree species to areas where they have been cut down.

TRY THIS AT HOME!

Photograph insects on plants and birds eating fruit and seeds. Think about why certain insects and birds might be associated with specific plant species.

Lisa Schulte Moore

PRAIRIE STRIPS

A NATURE LOVER

Lisa Schulte Moore grew up in Wisconsin, where she loved camping and visiting her great-grandmother's farm outside of her hometown of Eau Claire. After high school, she attended the University of Wisconsin, Eau Claire to study biology. "From there," she says, "it was kind of just following my interests and passions from one question to another." Her curiosity led her to northern Minnesota, where she did research for a master's degree, studying bird populations affected by wildfires and logging.

BUILDING BRIDGES

Eventually, she completed a PhD in forestry at UW and took a job with the U.S. Forest Service. While she was there, she learned that wildlife biologists and foresters sometimes had problems talking to each other, which makes it harder for everyone to do their jobs of conserving the forest. Realizing the importance of communication, Lisa decided to build bridges between groups who had different goals and priorities as part of her work going forward.

THE CORN BELT

In 2003, Lisa joined the faculty at Iowa State University, in Ames, Iowa, as a landscape ecologist with a goal of making agriculture work for both people and the planet. Iowa lies in the heart of America's Corn Belt, which was first inhabited by a number of tribes, including Dakota, Ho-Chunk, Ioway, Otoe, Illiniwek, Meskwaki, Omaha, and Sauk. When the U.S. government forced the Indigenous people off the land in the 1800s, most of it was settled as farmland.

RUNOFF

Unfortunately, farming can be harmful to the environment. Plowing up prairie to plant crops destroys ecosystems where pollinators, birds, and other animals live. Fertilizer and chemicals that are sprayed on crops to kill insects and stop weeds from growing run off the plants, into the soil, and make their way into the water supply. Lisa understands that while humans need the food, fiber, and fuel produced by agriculture, we must find ways to protect the environment.

PRAIRIE STRIPS

Lisa points out that where corn and soybeans are grown, the fields are bare for most of the year. Without roots holding it down, the soil is vulnerable to erosion by wind and water. Pollution from erosion moves into streams and rivers, ruining the water quality all the way from the Mississippi River to the Gulf of Mexico. Farm fields can also produce greenhouse gases. A prairie strip is an agricultural conservation technique that uses native grasses and plants planted in farm fields to help build soil and clean up rainwater.

CLEANER WATER, BETTER SOIL

Prairie strips also help keep fertilizer and other chemicals out of waterways while providing a habitat for native wildlife and pollinators. Lisa and her team have shown that by covering 10 percent of a crop field with prairie strips, they can keep 95 percent more of the soil in that field, 77 percent more phosphorus, and 70 percent more nitrogen, so less fertilizer is needed.

IN TODAY'S WORLD

Dr. Lisa Schulte Moore hopes that what scientists and farmers in Iowa are learning about using native plants to increase production and decrease environmental damage will someday be used in farms around the world.

* ECOLOGY *

TRY THIS AT HOME!

Trace the metal cap on a mason jar lid on brown paper. Cut a 0.2-inch (0.5-cm) hole in the center of the paper and then cut a line to the hole. Using pipe cleaners (chenille sticks) make a model of a small prairie plant with long roots. Slide it into the center of the brown paper circle so the roots go down. Put the roots into the mason jar and screw a ring lid on, so that the plant sits on top of the jar.

Nadya Mason

CONDUCTIVITY/CARBON

POKING AT ANT HILLS

From the time she was young, Nadya Mason has been interested in the world around her. As a child, she loved nature and satisfied her curiosity by running around picking fruit from trees and poking at anthills with sticks. Born in New York City, she lived in Brooklyn until she was six. Her family then moved to Washington D.C. and later to Houston, Texas.

A WORLD-CLASS GYMNAST

An exceptionally talented athlete, Nadya ran track and was a gymnast on the United States National team. In addition to sports, she was an excellent student who became interested in math at a young age. It wasn't until she had an opportunity to work in a biochemistry lab that she discovered her love of hands-on science and realized for the first time that it was possible to make science her career.

ATOMIC AMBITIONS

After high school, she went to Harvard University, where she took as many science and math classes as she could. Soon Nadya discovered that she likes physics the best. The science of atoms, the building blocks of matter, described the world in a way she understood and connected with. Her parents were supportive of the idea that Nadya would be a physicist and encouraged her to pursue her dreams.

A PROFESSOR

After getting her bachelor's degree at Harvard, she continued her studies at Stanford University, where she received her doctoral degree. Dr. Mason returned to Harvard to do some post-doctoral research before becoming an assistant professor and then a full professor at the University of Illinois Urbana-Champaign. Besides doing research there, she loves working with her students.

ELECTRON INTERACTIONS

Dr. Mason's laboratory focuses on how charged particles called electrons move through different materials, how they interact with each other, and why they conduct electricity the way that they do. She's especially interested in how electrons behave in very thin layers or small quantities of different materials. Nadya explains, "we work with carbon nanotubes that are just one-billionth of a meter in diameter but up to centimeters long; think of them as the tiniest wires you can make."

HANDS-ON THINKING

Dr. Mason is passionate about diversity issues that affect the scientific community. She works hard as a science communicator to encourage everyone to follow their interests in science, rather than being intimated by it. Dr. Mason gave a TED talk in 2019 titled "How to spark your creativity, scientifically," and said that "hands-on thinking (through experimentation) connects our understanding and even our vitality to the physical world and the things that we use." She has won several awards, including the American Physical Society's Maria-Goeppert Mayer Award, and was a general counselor to the American Physical Society (APS) and chair of the APS Committee on Minorities.

IN TODAY'S WORLD

Dr. Mason's research on electron movement through very small quantities of material could have an enormous impact on modern technology, such as the computer industry.

TRY THIS AT HOME!

Use a graphite pencil to scribble a solid rectangle on some paper. Stick a piece of clear wrapping tape to the graphite and lift the tape up. With a second piece of tape, lift graphite from the first piece of tape. Repeat several times with new pieces of tape, adhering them to white paper after lifting graphite. Photograph the tape. Zoom in to observe the successively thinner layers you made.

Danielle Lee

PATTERN RECOGNITION/SCIENCE COMMUNICATION

LIGHTNING BUGS

Danielle N. Lee grew up in South Memphis, Tennessee. Her biological father was a musician and her step-father, who married her mom when she was eight years old, was a tractor-trailer tire repairman. Until she married, Danielle's mother worked for Memphis Parks Commission and raised Danielle with the help of her family in a big multigenerational household. Because of her mom's job, Danielle spent lots of time outdoors, exploring woods and fields. Looking for four-leaf clovers trained her eyes to see patterns. She also loved collecting lightning bugs and making garlands from dandelions and clover grass flowers.

LOOKING FOR PATTERNS

Even as a child, Danielle was fascinated by animal behavior. When flocks of birds moved across the sky, she studied the patterns in their movements and won-dered whether their flight patterns were deliberate or whether they were trying to decide which bird to follow. She was never bored. During her free time, Danielle read books, listened to music, and did crafts. She enjoyed school and was good at it, but sometimes got in trouble for talking to her friends too much. Her teachers might have been surprised to discover that Danielle's excellent communication skills would come in handy later, when she became a professor.

A PROFESSOR

Danielle earned her bachelor's degree from Tennessee Technical University in 1996. At first, she wanted to go to veterinary school, but that didn't work out. Luckily, she started to study how small mammals called voles use their sense of smell and fell in love with the disci-pline of mammalogy. She got a master's degree from the University of Memphis and then a PhD in biology from the University of Missouri–St. Louis. Today, Dr. Lee teaches mammalogy (the study of mammals) and urban ecology at Southern Illinois University–Edwardsville. The focus of her current research is the behavior of African giant pouched rats, and she loves traveling to Tanzania to do field studies.

A SCIENCE COMMUNICATOR

Dr. Danielle N. Lee is well known for her ability to excite people about science. She does outreach to the public on social media, but she is especially passion-ate about her work as a role model and educator for underserved audiences. As a woman of color in science, she has faced extraordinary challenges and persevered. Dr. Lee has received many honors for her work, especially for encouraging minority participa-tion in Science, Technology, Engineering, and Math (STEM) fields. She is a 2015 TED Fellow and a 2107 National Geographic Emerging Explorer.

THE FOUR-LEAF CLOVER

The logo for Dr. Lee's laboratory is the four-leaf clover. Each leaf is associated with a word: Behavior, Ecology, Justice, and Outreach. The study of science depends on observation, and the symbol reminds people who work with her that a multitude of perspectives are essential. She says that the clover represents why we need different perspectives: just as different patterns stand out to different individuals looking at the exact same field of clovers, a multitude of viewpoints bring the big picture into sharper focus.

IN TODAY'S WORLD

Research on mammals and animal behavior is essen-tial to gaining insight into everything from economics to human health and wildlife conservation. Modern scientists, such as Dr. Lee, understand that it is essen-tial to communicate with the public to gain support for research and to inspire future scientists.

TRY THIS AT HOME!
Hone your pattern recognition skills by hunting for four-leaf clovers. Clover plants are part of the genus *Trifolium*, which means three leaves, but sometimes the DNA in clover undergoes genetic mutation and grows an extra leaflet.

Raychelle Burks

COLORIMETRIC SENSORS

CALIFORNIA KID

Growing up in California, Raychelle Burks loved going to the library and solving mysteries alongside the sleuths of her favorite detective stories. Her family spent hours having long discussions about books and movies, which fueled her curiosity about popular culture. As she grew, their conversations around television shows such as *Star Trek* inspired her to think critically about what she observed in the world around her.

SUPER SLEUTH

Raychelle's grandmother had introduced her to Agatha Christie, and she was drawn to the observant characters who assembled information in an orderly way to piece together a possible scenario. When she was a teenager, a visit to a forensic science lab showed her how scientific equipment and chemical tests could be used to lead investigators to discoveries about crimes. She realized that science was a vehicle that could turn her passion for solving mysteries into a career.

REAL-LIFE TRICORDER

After pursuing her education, Dr. Burks spent a few years working in a crime lab before returning to academia. Today, she is a professor of chemistry who studies colorimetric sensors for chemical identity and concentration determination. She uses forensic science research to help reveal clues, doubling up as a science communication superhero when she's not busy with molecular sleuthing in her laboratory.

AWARDS

Dr. Burks was awarded the 2019 Mindlin Foundation Science Communication Prize and the 2020 American Chemical Society James T. Grady-James H. Stack Award for Interpreting Chemistry for the Public. In 2019 she was selected as an AAAS If/Then Ambassador by the American Association for the Advancement of Science and the Lyda Hill Philanthropies.

SCI-COMM SUPERHERO

As a science communicator and role model for aspiring scientists, Dr. Burks uses popular culture as a positive space for discussions about society, science, and stereotypes. In the classroom, online, and beyond, she works to ignite appreciation of chemistry through hands-on projects and pop culture references. Burks helped create and organize *SciPop Talks!*, a popular talk series blending science and pop culture. She appears regularly on television, podcasts, and at genre conventions, and she owns a cheweenie, which is a cross between a dachshund and a chihuahua.

IN TODAY'S WORLD

The chemical sensor Dr. Burks is working to develop in her lab is astonishingly similar to the fictional tricorder on *Star Trek*, which is also a hand-held device used to scan the environment. Her current research efforts are focused on the design of sensing systems that can identify chemical clues tied to crime and uses smartphones, laptops, and tablets as scientific analytical devices.

TRY THIS AT HOME!

Download a colorimeter app on a device. Use the app to detect the red, green, and blue of different liquids. Think about how you could use the app to detect the presence of certain chemicals in a liquid.

Lesley de Souza

CONSERVATION BIOLOGY

ICHTHYOLOGY

Born in 1977, Lesley de Souza grew up exploring forests and creeks in the southeastern United States and on her family's farm in Brazil. As a child, Lesley and her little brother spent hours on end in forests and creeks. In college, she fell in love with fieldwork, which allowed her to continue exploring streams and rivers. She went on to graduate school and got a PhD in neotropical ichthyology (the study of fish in Central and South America).

THE WORLD'S LUNGS

Lesley's fascination with fish took her to the Amazon Basin and a region called the Guiana Shield in South America, all part of the Amazon rain forest, the largest, most diverse tropical rain forest on Earth. Many people refer to the Amazon as the world's lungs because its trees and plants play an essential role in keeping our atmosphere stable and breathable. The Amazon is a biodiversity hot spot, containing thousands of keystone species whose populations keep ecosystems healthy.

ARAPAIMA

Working with Indigenous people who understand their environment better than anyone else, Lesley studies a fish called arapaima, which can grow up to 10 feet (3 m) long and are strong enough to break your bones if you don't handle them correctly. By installing tiny radio transmitters in the fish, she tracks their movements as they migrate into the flooded forest during the rainy season.

A RAIN FOREST ECOSYSTEM

Lesley says, "There's no way to separate what's happening underwater from the top of the forest canopy. The macaws perched on top of the giant trees are dependent on the fish swimming in the river and vice versa. The river brings nutrients into the soils that are absorbed through the roots and permeate the entire landscape . . . fish feed upon the fruits that fall from the trees."

CONSERVATION FOR THE FUTURE

Like many scientists, Lesley is deeply concerned about ecological destruction in the Amazon. Logging and mining are threatening the fragile ecosystems. Cutting down trees and digging for gold pollutes the air and water and destroys waterways. In addition to studying fish, Lesley is interested in working with the Indigenous people and governments of the places she studies to create conservation areas. This helps to ensure a healthy future for the water, the land, and the people who live there.

IN TODAY'S WORLD

Dr. Lesley de Souza understands that it is essential to address environmental issues on a local level by working closely with governments and people who live in threatened ecosystems. Every ecosystem plays an important role in the larger ecosystem that is Earth.

* ECOLOGY *

TRY THIS AT HOME!

Make a terrarium! Fill the bottom of a large, clear container with gravel, charcoal, dried moss, and soil. Add plants and water. Cover the container with a lid or plastic wrap so water will evaporate, condense, and drip back into the soil.

Ayana Elizabeth Johnson

MARINE CONSERVATION/PUBLIC POLICY

A GLASS-BOTTOM BOAT

Ayana Elizabeth Johnson was born in Brooklyn, New York, in 1980, and grew up there. Ayana had always been interested in animals and spent hours digging up worms in her backyard. When she was five, Ayana fell in love with the ocean. Her family had taken a trip to Florida and ventured out in a glass-bottom boat. Staring down through the transparent floor, she was captivated by the magical coral reef below. By the time Ayana was ten, she also wanted to be a lawyer so that she could help people who were fighting for social justice.

BETTER FISH TRAPS

After high school, she studied environmental science and public policy at Harvard University. While pursuing her PhD in marine biology at the University of California's Scripps Institution, Ayana traveled to the Caribbean islands of Curacao and Bonaire to do research. Working with local fishermen and divers, she redesigned fish traps to reduce bycatch, which are fish caught by accident.

COLLABORATION

The collaboration was a success, and the new traps reduced bycatch by around 80 percent, allowing fishermen to catch what they needed while keeping other fish in the coral reef ecosystems safe. Ayana's work on the islands convinced her more than ever that she wanted to take an active role in conservation. She then went on to work with the people of the island of Barbuda as they created their own marine regulations.

CHANGE MAKER

In 2016, Ayana moved back to Brooklyn, where she worked with Greenpeace to protect coral reefs and with the World Wildlife Fund. She started a think tank for coastal cities called the Ocean Collective. She also worked on an ocean-centric plan for reducing the amount of carbon we put into the atmosphere, and launched a podcast called How to Save a Planet.

ENVIRONMENTAL JUSTICE

Ayana points out that environmental protection is a justice issue, saying, "If you think about the rates of asthma in inner-city communities that are near power plants or exposed to other types of pollution, it's a lot higher. And when we think about immigration, and how a lot of migration is now driven by climate change, that becomes a social justice issue that was triggered by the impacts on communities that did the least to emit the carbon to cause the problem."

RETURNING THE FAVOR

As a science communicator, Ayana likes to point out the role played by the ocean in slowing climate change. She says, "The ocean has already absorbed about 30 percent of the excess CO_2 that we've trapped by burning fossil fuels. And the ocean has already absorbed 93 percent of the heat that we've trapped. And so the ocean is trying its best to buffer us from our worst. We need to return the favor."

IN TODAY'S WORLD

To protect the ocean, Dr. Ayana Elizabeth Johnson suggests avoiding plastic containers, because plastic waste often ends up polluting the ocean. Keep your carbon footprint small by walking, biking, and using public transportation. Carpooling also reduces the amount of carbon dioxide gas that is soaked up by the ocean.

TRY THIS AT HOME!

To illustrate how excess carbon dioxide in the atmosphere affects ocean water, boil red cabbage in water. Strain and save the purple juice, which will turn pink in an acidic solution. Add $1/4$ cup (85 g) tap water to $1/4$ cup of the juice and look for a color change. Next, add $1/4$ cup carbonated water to $1/4$ cup of cabbage juice. It will turn slightly pink, because when carbon dioxide dissolves in water, carbonic acid is produced.

Jodie Darquea Arteaga

BYCATCH REDUCTION

A DIVERSE LANDSCAPE

Jodie Darquea Arteaga was born in Ecuador, a country on South America's west coast that sits on both sides of the equator and encompasses the Andean highlands, the Amazon jungle, and the Galápagos Islands. When she was sixteen, Jodie went to study biology at the State University, where her research involved learning to breed and harvest a species of fish called almaco jack.

FROM SHRIMP FARMING TO RESEARCH

While Jodie dreamed of getting a master's degree in marine biology, it was difficult for students who were not from wealthy families to advance in the education system, so she went to work for the shrimp industry. However, she was more interested in conservation than farming shrimp and went to work for Equilibrio Azul, a nonprofit research and conservation organization.

ON-BOARD OBSERVATION

Jodie's new position involved accompanying Ecuadorian fishermen on their boats to observe bycatch in small fishing fleets. Bycatch occurs when nontarget species such as dolphins, birds, and turtles get tangled up in fishing lines and nets. These accidental entanglements often result in the death of the bycatch. Jodie monitored hundreds of these fishing trips, documenting the species and bycatch conditions.

SCRIPPS INSTITUTE OF OCEANOGRAPHY

Jodie also fought hard to protect endangered birds like the waved albatross and worked for the government as chief protector of a marine-protected area called the Pelado. Then, to continue her education, she took two years of intensive English classes and applied to graduate school. Her dream came true when she was accepted to the master's program at the University of California's Scripps Institution of Oceanography. The program was difficult, but she persisted, and in 2016 she received her master's degree in advanced studies in marine biodiversity and conservation.

ECUADOR ECOLOGICAL WORLD

Today, Jodie Darquea Arteaga is an associate research professor at Ecuador's State University of the Santa Elena Peninsula, serving as a mentor to other young biologists. She is part of the team at Ecuador Ecological World, a nonprofit organization dedicated to conservation and the sustainable management of coastal marine resources for the benefit of coastal communities.

SAVING SEA TURTLES

Before Jodie's work began, there was no documentation of bycatch in Ecuador. Today, alongside other partners, she and her team continue to work with local fishermen. Jodie's latest project provides LEDs (very bright lights) to fishermen to reduce the number of sea turtles that get tangled in their nets. Jodie, who has always worked hard to achieve her dreams, now has a daughter named Maya to accompany her on her expeditions.

IN TODAY'S WORLD

Sustainable fishing reduces bycatch to protect ecosystems and keep fish populations healthy. When buying seafood, look for the blue Marine Stewardship Council (MSC) logo. The MSC is an international organization whose mission is to end overfishing and ensure seafood is caught sustainably.

TRY THIS AT HOME!

Fill a bowl with water. Add a variety of plastic fish, or small fruit like cranberries, blueberries, or grapes, to the water. Using an aquarium net or a sieved kitchen spoon, try to scoop up one kind of fish or fruit without catching any others.

Chanda Prescod-Weinstein

COSMOLOGY

A BASEBALL FAN

Chanda Prescod-Weinstein was born in the El Sereno neighborhood of Los Angeles, California, where the Tongva village of Otsungna stood until Spanish colonizers arrived around 1770. El Sereno is near Dodger Stadium, and as a kid Chanda became a huge fan of the Dodgers baseball team. In addition to dreaming of becoming a professional baseball player, she played piano, flute, and saxophone.

READING, DANCING, AND MATH

When she was young, Chanda loved practicing her multiplication tables. Soon, she became comfortable with mathematics, which is the language of physics. In high school, books such as Stephen Hawking's *A Brief History of Time* got her excited about black holes and the building blocks of the universe. In addition to reading and studying, Chanda attended a performing arts school, where she trained as a dancer in both modern dance and jazz.

FRESHMAN PHYSICS

Chanda attended Harvard University, where she earned degrees in physics and astronomy. Despite finding her freshman physics class somewhat boring, she later realized that the simple experiments they did in class built a solid foundation that would help her solve more interesting and complicated problems in the future.

A MENTOR

Most of Chanda's physics professors and classmates were white men, so she had to create her own vision of herself as a physicist. When she was almost done with her undergraduate degree, she finally met a Black woman with a doctoral degree in physics— Dr. Nadya Mason, who became a role model and a mentor. Chanda got a master's degree in astronomy, a doctoral degree in theoretical physics, and a job as an assistant professor in physics and core faculty in women's and gender studies at the University of New Hampshire.

UNIVERSAL QUESTIONS

As a theoretical physicist, Dr. Prescod-Weinstein uses math to solve the mysteries of the universe. Scientists think that the universe contains a lot of invisible stuff, called dark energy and dark matter, along with "a tiny smidgeon of everyday stuff like us." Dr. Prescod-Weinstein uses ideas from physics and astronomy to learn more about dark matter and address questions about how everything in the universe "got to the be the way it is."

AN AUTHOR AND AN ACTIVIST

Besides studying particles physics, Dr. Prescod-Weinstein is a popular science communicator and an activist for equality in science. She is a Pilates instructor, loves *Star Trek*, and does research on feminist science studies. Her book *The Disordered Cosmos: A Journey into Dark Matter, Spacetime, and Dreams Deferred* explores these ideas. She has received several prestigious awards for her work in particle physics, astrophysics, and astronomy.

IN TODAY'S WORLD

Scientists are currently using data collected by ground-based and space observatories to study the light coming from 35 million galaxies. They hope to reconstruct how the universe has been expanding over the last 11 billion years. Ideally, this work will help us understand the nature of dark energy.

TRY THIS AT HOME!

Make a batch of bread dough or pizza dough. Add poppy seeds, sesame seeds, or spices such as oregano to the dough to represent galaxies. As the dough rises, the seeds and spices will move apart. This shows how as the universe expands outward in all directions, galaxies and other cosmic objects move away from each other.

Rae Wynn-Grant

CARNIVORE ECOLOGY/ANIMAL BEHAVIOR

URBAN CHILDHOOD

Rae Wynn-Grant grew up in big cities. Born in San Francisco, she spent most of her childhood in California. Her mother is a writer and her father is an architect, so it surprised everyone when she decided to be a wildlife biologist. As a kid, she remembers being fascinated by television shows about wild animals. When she was a teenager, Rae dreamed about hosting her own nature show on *National Geographic*. In middle school and high school, she struggled with traditional tests and found math and science challenging, but Rae loved the things she was learning about the natural world and didn't allow less-than-perfect grades stand in her way.

ENVIRONMENTAL STUDIES

After high school, Rae attended Emory University where she learned about conservation biology, which focuses on protecting and restoring the diversity of life on Earth. She didn't get to see her first wild animal until she traveled to East Africa when she was nineteen years old. Rae studied for a master's degree in environmental studies from Yale University and then got a doctorate degree, studying how carnivores adapt (change) their behavior to adjust to landscapes altered by humans.

LIONS AND LEMURS AND BEARS

Rae loves bears. "They're just like people," she said in an interview with National Geographic Explorers at Work. "They just love to hang out." After finishing her PhD in ecology and evolution from Columbia University, she did research called a post-doctoral for the American Museum of Natural History, studying the behavior and habitat of grizzly bears in Montana.

Today, she studies bears in the mountains of Nevada and New York and does research on lions in Tanzania and lemurs in Madagascar. Dr. Wynn-Grant is interested in learning how animals, such as lions, change their movement and hunting patterns when humans live nearby. Her science work is dedicated to helping people and carnivores coexist peacefully all around the world.

A DREAM-COME-TRUE

Rae currently works as a large carnivore ecologist for the National Geographic Society and studies carnivore conservation around the world. She is a Visiting Scientist at the American Museum of Natural History and a professor at Columbia University and Johns Hopkins University. Dr. Wynn-Grant does some of her most important work as a science communicator, making environmental science accessible to broad and diverse audiences. Rae wants to show urban kids that they have a place doing work like hers. "Don't confuse performance with passion" is her motto. Dr. Rae Wynn-Grant is living proof that passion and hard work can make dreams come true.

IN TODAY'S WORLD

As Earth's population grows, people are moving into the habitat of wild animals. The work of Dr. Rae Wynn-Grant and other conservation ecologists is essential to the well-being of humans and animals. Her dream of hosting a nature show came true in 2023, when she became the co-host of *Mutual of Omaha's Wild Kingdom*.

Burçin Mutlu-Pakdil

GALAXIES

ISTANBUL

Burçin Mutlu-Pakdil was born in the Turkish city of Istanbul, which lies in both Europe and Asia. Istanbul is an ancient, famous city that went by the names Byzantium and Constantinople in the past. Burçin's grandparents never learned to read or write and her parents were not able to pursue an education beyond the fifth grade due to financial issues. Despite those challenges, her parents believed strongly in education.

REACHING FOR THE STARS

In middle school, Burçin became interested in physics when she read a book about Albert Einstein. She had always liked looking at the stars, and now she wanted to learn more about them. Her family encouraged her to study physics, and despite the disapproval of some friends and relatives, Burçin left Istanbul to attend Bilkent University in Ankara, Turkey.

FOCUSING ON PHYSICS

When Burçin arrived at college, one of her male professors told her it was crazy for a woman to leave her hometown to study physics. At the university, she was not allowed to wear her hijab and constantly battled prejudice. Despite all the obstacles, she refused to let anything stand in her way and remained focused on her passion until she graduated. Burçin then moved to the United States to study astrophysics, earning a master's degree from Texas Tech and a PhD from the University of Minnesota. Today, Dr. Burçin Mutlu-Pakdil studies the most mysterious objects in the universe, at the University of Chicago.

BURCIN'S GALAXY

Burçin and her research team first spotted a very peculiar object in the background while studying another galaxy. At first glance, it was a beautiful celestial object with a ball of yellowish stars surrounded by a single ring of blue stars. Galaxies like these are extremely rare. When looking at the galaxy in different lights, they unexpectedly discovered an additional unique structure—a second inner ring, making this galaxy the first example of an elliptical galaxy with two symmetric rings. This unique, beautiful elliptical galaxy, 359 million light years away, is now commonly called Burçin's Galaxy.

UNIVERSAL MYSTERIES

Dr. Burçin Mutlu-Pakdil uses some of the largest telescopes in the world. She travels to locations such as Hawaii and Chile to collect data and study scientific mysteries, such as dark matter and how the faintest and smallest galaxies form and evolve in the universe. In addition to having a galaxy named after her, she has won many awards for her work in physics and is a role model for young scientists. She says, "I do not want to blend in; I want to stand out as stars do, so I fought against all these stereotypes and worked hard to live beyond the labels."

IN TODAY'S WORLD

Our galaxy, the Milky Way, formed around 14 billion years ago, attracting heavy elements that came together to form the sun, and our planet. Using powerful tools such as the Keck telescopes in Hawaii, astronomers can see the light from 100 billion other galaxies. Each of these galaxies contains 100 billion stars. By using spectra collected by the telescopes, astronomers are discovering what the galaxies are made of. They hope to learn more about the universe and whether there may be other galaxies containing planets that could support life.

TRY THIS AT HOME!

Tie a Wiffle ball onto either end of a 3-foot (0.9-m) cord or thin rope to represent two galaxies connected by gravity. Cover the balls with duct tape to make them heavier. Holding the galaxy model by one end, swing the rope a few times and let it fly through the air to see how two galaxies might move together through space.

ACKNOWLEDGMENTS

I'm extremely grateful to each of the helpful, talented people who collaborated to put this book together: my long-time acquiring editor Jonathan Simcosky; art designer Heather Godin, editorial project manager Gabrielle Bethancourt-Hughes; editorial intern Gabrielle Cruz, design intern Meigan English, marketing managers Angela Corpus and Mel Schuit; and the entire design and editing team. I'm lucky to have such a skilled, supportive group to work with. Thank you to Kelly Anne Dalton, who brings the scientists in these pages to life so beautifully, and to my literary agent Victoria Wells Arms. Special thanks to each of the scientists who took time from their busy schedules to answer my questions and tell me stories from the field. And a shout-out to my family and friends, who keep me laughing and learning every day.

ABOUT THE AUTHOR

Liz Heinecke has loved science since she was old enough to inspect her first butterfly. After working in molecular biology research for ten years and getting her master's degree, Liz left the lab to kick off a new chapter in her life. Soon she found herself sharing her love of science with her three kids, journaling their science adventures on KitchenPantryScientist.com. Her desire to spread her enthusiasm for science to others soon led to regular TV appearances, speaking engagements, and her books: *Kitchen Science Lab for Kids* (Quarry Books), *Outdoor Science Lab for Kids* (Quarry Books), *STEAM Lab for Kids* (Quarry Books), *Star Wars Maker Lab* (DK), *Kitchen Science Lab for Kids: Edible Edition* (Quarry Books), *The Kitchen Pantry Scientist: Chemistry for Kids* (Quarry Books), *The Kitchen Pantry Scientist: Biology for Kids* (Quarry Books), *Sheet Pan Science* (Quarry Books), *The Padawan Cookbook* (Insight Editions), *The Kitchen Pantry Scientist: Ecology* (Quarry Books), and *RADIANT: The Dancer, The Scientist, and a Friendship Forged in Light*, an adult nonfiction narrative about Marie Curie and Loie Fuller (Grand Central Publishing). Most days, you'll find Liz at home in Minnesota. She graduated from Luther College with a BA in art and received her master's degree in bacteriology from the University of Wisconsin, Madison.

ABOUT THE ILLUSTRATOR

Kelly Anne Dalton is an artist, illustrator, and storyteller living in the wild mountains of Montana. Her elegant and enchanting work can be found on everything from board books to middle grade novel covers, home decor and gift products, and stationery lines. When not drawing, daydreaming, and creating new stories and characters, Kelly Anne can be found trail running in the forests near her home.

INDEX

A

Almeida, June, 64
Arteaga, Jodie Darquea, 103

B

Ball, Alice, 32
Bassi, Laura, 15
Bath, Patricia, 72
Bergstrom, Dana, 87
biology
  agar growth medium, 19
  agglutination, 64
  agrostology, 27
  animal behavior, 107
  carnivore ecology, 107
  cataract surgery, 72
  coronaviruses, 64
  houseflies, 24
  illustration, 12
  lambda phage, 59
  pattern recognition, 95
  plant collection/identification, 28
  public health, 24
  replica plating, 59
  termites, 56
  zoology, 56
Blodgett, Katharine Burr, 36
Buck, Linda, 83
Burks, Raychelle, 96
Burnell, Jocelyn Bell, 80

C

Carson, Rachel, 47
Chase, Mary Agnes, 27
chemistry
  colorimetric sensors, 96
  crystallography, 76
  DNA structure, 55
  elemental extraction, 23
  fragrance distillation, 11
  medicinal plant compounds, 63
  molecular sieves, 60
  nuclear shell model, 43
  olfactory chemistry, 83
  organic compounds, 51
  organic separation, 32
  ribosome structure, 68
  surface tension, 20
  ultraviolet light, 51
Collins, Margaret S., 56
Cori, Gerty, 35
Curie, Marie, 23

D

Darden, Christine, 75
Datta, Aparajita, 88

E

Earle, Sylvia, 67
ecology
  Antarctic research, 87
  carbon reduction, 100
  carnivore ecology, 107
  conservation biology, 99
  environmental contaminants, 47
  forest ecology, 84
  green belt movement, 71
  greenhouse gases, 16
  oceanography, 67, 103
  parasitology, 40
  prairie strips, 91
  seed dispersal, 88
Etter, Margaret Cairns, 76

F

Flanigen, Edith, 60
Foote, Eunice Newton, 16
Franklin, Rosalind, 55

G

Goeppert-Mayer, Maria, 43

H

Harrison, Anna Jane, 51
Henry, Dora Priaulx, 40
Hesse, Fanny, 19

J

Johnson, Ayana Elizabeth, 100

K

Kimmerer, Robin Wall, 84

L

Lederberg, Esther, 59
Lee, Danielle, 95

M

Maathai, Wangari, 71
Mason, Nadya, 92
Meitner, Lise, 31
Merian, Maria Sibylla, 12
Mexía, Ynés, 28
Moore, Lisa Schulte, 91
Mutlu-Pakdil, Burçin, 108

P

Payne-Gaposchkin, Cecilia, 39
Payne-Scott, Ruby, 52
physics
  aerospace engineering, 44
  aircraft wing design, 75
  carbon, 92
  conductivity, 92
  cosmology, 104
  electricity, 15
  films, 36
  galaxies, 108
  illusion transmitter, 79
  non-reflective glass, 36
  nuclear fission, 31
  pulsars, 80
  star spectroscopy, 39
  sunspots, 52
  symmetry, 48
Picotte, Susan La Flesche, 24
Pockels, Agnes, 20
Prescod-Weinstein, Chanda, 104

R

Ross, Mary Golda, 44

S

Souza, Lesley de, 99

T

Tapputi-Belatikallim, 11
Thomas, Valerie L., 79

W

Wu, Chien-Shiung, 48
Wynn-Grant, Rae, 107

Y

Yonath, Ada, 68
Youyou, Tu, 63